LEDGE

lucation

CONDITIONS
OF
KNOWLEDGE

AN INTRODUCTION TO EPISTEMOLOGY AND EDUCATION

ISRAEL SCHEFFLER

THE UNIVERSITY OF CHICAGO PRESS
CHICAGO AND LONDON

The author gratefully acknowledges the cooperation of the following publishers for permission to reprint material in this book:

American Philosophical Association: for excerpt from "Rational Action"
by Carl G. Hempel. *Proceedings and Addresses of the American Philosophical
Association,* **XXXV.**

Harper & Row, Publishers, Inc.: for excerpts from *The Concept of Mind* by
Gilbert Ryle.

The Clarendon Press, Oxford: for excerpts from *Philosophical Papers* by
J. L. Austin. Reprinted by permission of The Clarendon Press, Oxford.

David McKay Co., Inc., formerly Longmans, Green and Co.: for excerpts
from *Pragmatism* by William James. Permission to reprint granted by
Paul R. Reynolds.

Hutchinson & Co. (Publishers) Ltd.: for British rights for excerpts from
The Concept of Mind by Gilbert Ryle.

The University of Chicago Press, Chicago 60637
The University of Chicago Press, Ltd., London

© 1965 by Israel Scheffler

All rights reserved. Published 1965
University of Chicago edition 1978
Midway reprint 1983
Printed in the United States of America

ISBN: 0-226-73669-5
LCN: 78-54987

In memory of my father
Leon Scheffler
1885 – 1964

TABLE OF CONTENTS

PREFACE

Conditions of Knowledge is intended as an introduction to epistemology, from the perspective of education. I have tried to present
some of the major issues in the theory of knowledge, as developed
particularly in recent philosophy, and to deal analytically with these
issues in the context of educational interests.

My approach has not been purely expository. I have selected
topics that have seemed to me both interesting and important, and
have expressed my own judgments in the course of my treatment.
My hope has been to engage the reader himself in the process of
philosophical reflection on the nature and conditions of knowledge,
to encourage him to develop his own solutions to the problems and
his own evaluation of their educational bearings.

I wish here to express my thanks to Mrs. Dorothy Spotts for
her typing, to Peter F. Carbone, Jr. for comments and help with
bibliography and footnotes, and to David Halfen, Mrs. Betty Leake,
and Miss Judy Gregg for editorial suggestions. I am grateful for
support from the William F. Milton Fund, which facilitated the
preparation of the manuscript.

Israel Scheffler

•

Epistemology and Education

•

PURPOSE OF THE BOOK

The development and transmission of knowledge are fundamental tasks of education, while analysis of its nature and warrant
falls to that branch of philosophy known as epistemology, or theory
of knowledge. An adequate educational philosophy must not only
address itself to epistemological problems in their general form but
must also strive to view these problems from the perspective of educational tasks and purposes.
It is this aim which defines the direction and emphasis of the
present book. In the conviction that epistemological analysis is itself
an important ingredient of educational philosophy, we shall investigate
selected issues in the general theory of knowledge, especially as they
arise in recent and contemporary discussions. Moreover, we shall
examine these issues throughout against a fixed background of educational interests, exploring whatever bearings they may appear to have
on the analysis of specifically educational concepts and considerations.
The book may thus be taken to be at once an introduction to the
theory of knowledge and an introduction to educational philosophy.
Perhaps it is best thought of as an introduction to epistemology in
educational perspective.

THREE PHILOSOPHIES OF KNOWLEDGE

It will be well to survey, at the very outset, some of the com-
plexities of our subject. For if the task of epistemology can be simply
put as the logical analysis of knowledge, knowledge is itself far from
simple. First of all, the range of the everyday concept of knowing

is very wide, including familiarity with things, places, persons, and subjects, competence in a variety of learned performances, and possession of ostensible truths on matters of fact as well as faith, the fallible items of science and everyday experience as well as the alleged certainties of mathematics and metaphysics.

Secondly, the concept of knowing is related in important ways to other fundamental and difficult ideas. It is, for example, closely associated with notions of understanding and controlling nature so as to sustain and enhance civilized life; it is also associated with ideas of contemplation, absorption, and appreciation, prized for themselves—ends rather than means of civilized life. In educational contexts, the term *knowledge* is frequently intended as embracing both sets of ideas: the accumulated skill and lore pertaining to technological control of the environment, and those intellectual arts and experiences whose value is intrinsic to themselves. *Knowledge*, in such contexts, marks the whole content of our intellectual heritage, which education is concerned to pass on to succeeding generations.

Finally, attributions of knowledge are not, in typical cases, simply descriptive of bodies of lore or types of experience; they express our standards, ideals, and tastes as to the scope and proper conduct of the cognitive arts. They reflect, for example, our conceptions of truth and evidence, our estimates of the possibilities of secure belief, our preferences among alternative strategies of investigation. To describe someone as knowing is as much to appraise and approve as it is to report. Correspondingly, education is concerned to transmit not only what we know, but our manner of knowing, that is, our approved standards of competence in performance, in inquiry, and in intellectual criticism.

It is hardly surprising, then, that the concept of knowledge should have given rise to a variety of traditions of full-blown philosophical interpretation. For not only does the mere breadth of the concept lend itself to alternative emphases, but its intimate association with variable ideals of civilization and with changing technologies and scientific models invites correspondingly varying evaluations. We shall sketch, by way of illustration, three broad philosophical approaches to knowledge, the rationalistic, the empiricistic, and the pragmatic.[1]

For the rationalistic tradition, mathematics is the model science. Mathematical truths are general and necessary, and may be established by deductive chains linking them with self-evident basic truths. Demonstration forges the chains, intuition discloses the basic truths. Intuition, moreover, guarantees each link in the chain of demonstration. Whoever understands a mathematical truth knows it to be necessary and not contingent on facts of nature. A diagram may well be used to *illustrate* a geometrical theorem, but it cannot be construed as *evidence for* the theorem. Should precise measurement of the diagram show that it failed to embody the relations asserted by the theorem, the latter would not be falsified. We should rather say that the physical diagram was only an approximation or a suggestion of the truth embodied in the theorem. Physical points have spread and physical lines have width, but mathematical points and lines are ideal, not physical objects—they can be understood, but not exemplified in the natural world. Natural objects only approximate, to a greater or lesser degree, the ideal objects of mathematics, and to the extent that they do approximate these ideal objects, they also can be understood. Statements, however, which *directly* describe natural objects are only more-or-less in character; they are contingent rather than necessary, dependent on the evidence of observed particulars for their substantiation, and subject to falsification through experience.

Mathematical truths are not dependent on experience, though an awareness of them may be suggested by experience. Mathematicians do not need laboratories or experiments; they conduct no surveys and collect no statistics. They work with pencil and paper only, and yet they arrive at the firmest of all truths, incapable of being overthrown by experience. In Plato's dialogue, *Meno*, an untutored slave boy is led, through a skillful series of questions centered around a diagram, to an acknowledgment of the geometrical truth that a double square is the square of the diagonal.[2] Plato, drawing upon such examples, supposes the source of genuine knowledge to be within, and the knowledge itself to be capable of elicitation by questioning and suggestion which merely draw the mind's attention to that which it already possesses. The ideal education, for Plato, is a mathematical education, in which the mind comes to an apprehension of necessary truths concerning ideal forms, and which equips the student to grasp the natural world as an approximate embodiment of these forms.

In the empiricistic tradition, natural science is taken as the basic model. Natural phenomena are revealed by experience; they are not disclosed by intuition, nor are their interrelationships derivable from self-evident axioms. A person deprived of visual experience from birth may be fully rational and in possession of his logical faculties, but he will be unable to intuit or even imagine the color green. Neither this color nor any other elementary phenomenal component is initially present in the mind, to be drawn up by introspection; it must be gained by observation in the course of experience. Furthermore, the relationships among elementary phenomena—their typical clustering and their patterning through time—cannot be inferred by logic from self-evident basic truths; they are natural associations tentatively projected as generalizations from our limited past experience. The mind, in Locke's phrase, is a *tabula rasa* (a blank slate) at birth, and it is dependent upon experience both for the content of its elementary ideas and for their interrelationships.

The mind must, of course, be construed as having the power to compare, combine, analyze, and generalize upon the materials furnished to it by experience, as well as the ability to perform logical operations upon its concepts. Mathematics may be understood to represent either "internal" logical relationships among concepts, or very abstract, though still empirical, generalizations based upon experience. In any event, all knowledge which reaches beyond the circle of the mind's own concepts and refers to the world must be based upon observation of what lies beyond, of what is not innate in the mind itself. The ideal education suggested by the empiricist view is one which supplies abundant and optimally ordered phenomenal experiences to the student so that his powers of observation and association may take hold and enable him to grasp the natural order among events. The ideal education, further, trains the student not only in proper logical habits but in traits requisite for learning from experience—accurate observation, reasonable generalization, willingness to revise or relinquish purported laws which fail to anticipate the actual course of events.

The pragmatic view stresses the experimental character of empirical science, putting great emphasis upon the active phases of experimentation. To learn something significant about the world, we must do more than operate logically upon basic truths that appear to us self-evident, and we must go beyond reasonable generalization of observed phenomenal patterns in our past experience. Experimentation involves active transformation of the environment, in a manner dictated by leading ideas put forward in response to problems and directed toward the resolution of these problems. The problem provides the occasion and enduring focus of experimental inquiry; it supplies the initial questions, furnishes controlling standards of relevance, and defines success in the undertaking. Thought provides hypothetical ideas in response to the problem, ideas which need not mirror past experience so long as they are directed to the questions at stake and are capable of providing *relevant* answers. These hypothetical ideas are tested in action; using them as instruments for controlled operations upon nature, the experimenter finds that not all of them are equally effective. Some raise expectations that are not fulfilled by experimental outcomes, others accurately foretell the responses of nature. In Dewey's words, the process is one of *trying and undergoing*—trying an idea in practice, and learning from the consequences undergone as a result of such trial.[3]

Mathematical knowledge is continuous with logic in the pragmatist's scheme. It is an apparatus useful for elaborating the import of hypothetical ideas, for showing their connections with practical consequences and exhibiting their mutual relationships. It does not itself tell us anything directly about the world, but in bringing order to our array of concepts and in generating their consequences, it serves as a regulative instrument of inquiry. Inquiry itself is action, but action regulated by logic, sparked by theory, and issuing in answers to motivating problems of practice. The process of learning from experience is thus an active process for the pragmatist. The mind is conceived neither as a deep well of necessary truths nor as a blank slate upon which experience writes. Rather, it is viewed as a capacity for active generation of ideas whose function it is to resolve the problems posed to an organism by its environment. The ideal education is thus one that connects general ideas with real problems and that stresses their practical bearings. It encourages imaginative theorizing by the student but at the same time insists upon control of such theorizing by the outcomes of active experimentation.

ALTERNATIVE QUESTIONS CONCERNING KNOWLEDGE

The three approaches just sketched exemplify certain of the contrasting emphases among broad philosophical interpretations of knowledge. They also serve to illustrate the variety of questions to which schools of interpretation have been addressed. Thus, each approach we have presented treats not only of the nature and warrant of knowledge, but also of its genesis and its proper development. It will be worthwhile to distinguish schematically several questions pertaining to knowledge, so that the main focus of our ensuing discussions may be clearly indicated.

First, we may consider the epistemological question: "What is knowledge?" To seek to answer this question is to strive for a general description or definition, a statement of criteria of knowledge which may serve to clarify its logical status. Secondly, there is the evaluative question: "What knowledge is most reliable or important?" To address oneself to this question is to ask for a classification of sorts of knowing and a ranking of these sorts by reference to some reasonable standard of worth. Thirdly, we may note the genetic question: "How does knowledge arise?" To answer this question is to give an account of the processes or mechanisms by which knowledge develops; it is, typically, to provide some model of the mind that may render learning processes intelligible. Fourthly, there is the methodological question: "How ought the search for knowledge to be conducted?" To answer this question is to offer some conception of proper methods to be employed in inquiry, together with a justification of these methods. Fifthly, we may consider the pedagogical question: "How is knowledge best taught?" To answer this question is to say how teaching ought ideally to proceed in the transmission of knowledge.

These questions have often been insufficiently distinguished from one another. It is, however, important to see that they are *logically distinct,* even though they are intimately related within broad philosophical interpretations and are all indeed essential for any comprehensive philosophy of education. We shall focus specifically on the epistemological question and shall not directly address ourselves to evaluative, genetic, methodological, or pedagogical issues. We shall, however, also attempt to relate the epistemological question, wherever this seems possible, to analyses of educational concepts and situations. In the next chapter, we shall introduce some general comparisons of cognitive and educational terms and discuss the ranges of these terms; we shall then present a definition of propositional knowledge which will serve as a basis for our discussion in later chapters.

•

CHAPTER ONE

Knowledge and Teaching

•

COGNITIVE AND EDUCATIONAL TERMS RELATED

How are the cognitive terms *knowing* and *believing* related to the educational terms *learning* and *teaching?* The question is not as simple as it may seem, and our consideration of it in this section will introduce several points of relevance throughout our discussions.

We might, as a result of attending to certain simple cases, suppose *learning that* to imply *knowing that*. If a student, for example, has *learned that* Boston is the capital of Massachusetts, we should normally say he has come to *know that* Boston is the capital of Massachusetts. Yet we cannot generalize from such cases that whenever a person X has learned that Q, he has come to know that Q.

Consider a student in some distant age or culture in which disease has been attributed to the action of evil spirits. Such a student may well have learned from his tutors that disease is caused by evil spirits, but we should not be willing to describe him as having come to know that disease is caused by evil spirits. *He* may, to be sure, have been perfectly willing to say "I *know* that evil spirits cause disease," but nonetheless *we* will not wish to describe him as having come to know that evil spirits cause disease, for we should then ourselves be admitting that evil spirits *do* cause disease. For us to say that some person knows that such and such is the case is, in general, for us to commit ourselves to the embedded substantive assertion that such and such *is* the case. Where such a commitment is repugnant to us, we will accordingly avoid attributing knowledge, though we may still attribute belief. In the present case, we will deny that the student in question has come to know that evil spirits cause disease, but we may safely describe him as having come to believe that evil spirits cause disease, for our belief attribution does *not* commit us to the substantive assertion in question. In our earlier example, by contrast, since we were perfectly willing to agree that Boston is the capital of Massachusetts, the stronger attribution of knowledge to the student did not commit us to an embedded substantive claim we found repugnant.

We are thus led to contrast *learning that* and *knowing that* in the following way: To say that someone has come to know that Q, commits us generally to the substantive assertion represented by "Q." For example, if we say of a pupil that he has come to know that Cornwallis surrendered at Yorktown, we are ourselves committed to the substantive assertion, "Cornwallis surrendered at Yorktown." To say that someone has learned that Q, does not so commit us; we are, in general, limited only to the claim that he has come to believe that Q.[1]

There are, to be sure, certain uses of *learning that* which do, in fact, commit us substantively in the manner we have been discussing. Consider the following statement, for example: "Reporters, after extensive investigation, learned that secret negotiations had been in progress for three weeks before the agreement was announced publicly." The force of "learned that" in this statement approximates that of "found out that" or "discovered that," which do commit us substantively. We may label such a use of "learn that," a *discovery use*, and contrast it with the *tutorial use*, in which the expression refers (without committing us substantively) to what people come to believe in consequence of schooling. The existence of the tutorial use suffices to show that a *learn that* attribution does not, in general, commit us to the embedded substantive assertion. And as we saw earlier, this is sufficient to *block* the generalization that what X has learned he has come to know, permitting only the weaker generalization that what X has learned he has come to believe.

The weaker generalization, in other words, unlike the stronger one, frees us from commitment to repugnant substantive claims in all those cases where we attribute *learning that* tutorially but reject the content learned. The student mentioned earlier may well be admitted to have learned, and to have believed, that evil spirits cause disease, but he cannot well be admitted to have come to know this. Suppose, now, that we consider all and only those cases where (i) X has learned that Q, and where (ii) we concur with the substantive assertion represented by "Q." Should we be willing in all these cases, at least, to say that X has indeed come to know (and not merely to believe) that Q?

This question raises a point of general importance regarding the attribution of knowledge: Some writers on the subject have recognized a weak and a strong sense of *know that*.[2] The answer to our question will depend on which sense we have in mind. In the weak sense, *knowing that* depends solely on having true belief; in the strong sense, it requires something further—for example, the ability to back up the belief in a relevant manner, to bring evidence in its support, or to show that one is in a position to know what it affirms. If we take the weak sense of *know that*, we shall then answer our question in the affirmative. If X has learned that Q and has therefore come to believe that Q, and if, further, we are willing to concur with the claim made by "Q" (i.e., to affirm it as true), we must acknowledge that X has come to believe truly, hence to know (in the weak sense) that Q.

If we take the strong sense of *know that*, however, we must answer our question in the negative. For a person may believe correctly or truly that Q, and yet lack the ability to provide adequate backing for his belief or to show that he is in a position to know that Q. Though he has learned that Q and has come to believe truly that Q, he will then not *really* know, or know in the strong sense, that Q. He has, for example, learned in school that $E = mc^2$, but cannot, unless he can supply suitable supporting reasons, be said to know (in the strong sense) that $E = mc^2$.

We may summarize our discussion to this point as follows: If X has learned that Q, he has come to believe that Q. If we deny "Q," we will directly rule out that X has also come to know that Q, no matter how well X is able to support "Q." On the other hand, if we grant that "Q" is true, it is not directly ruled out that we shall say X has come to know that Q. We shall, indeed, say this immediately if we employ the weak sense of *know*, but only upon the satisfaction of further conditions if we employ the strong sense of *know*.

Often, perhaps typically, however, we do not make a direct test to determine whether these further conditions have indeed been satisfied; we operate rather on general presumptions that seem to us plausible. The presumption that the relevant conditions have been satisfied varies, for example, with the difficulty, technicality, or complexity of the subject. Thus, it seemed quite natural to us earlier to say that a student who has learned that Boston is the capital of Massachusetts has indeed come to know this. Nor does this seem to be simply a result of using the weak sense of *know*. The question "He has learned it, but does he really know it?" springs less easily to our lips in this case than in the case of "$E = mc^2$." For what sort of complex technical backing could possibly be needed here? Granted that the strong sense of *know* is operative, we are more likely to presume, on general grounds, that a student who has learned a "simple" fact can support it appropriately than we are likely to make the same presumption for a relatively "complex" or technical affirmation.

Another source of variation seems to be the method by which the belief has been acquired. To have merely been made aware or informed by somebody that Q leaves open the practical possibility that one does not really know (in the strong sense) that Q, even where "Q" is true. To have found out for oneself that Q, lends greater credence to the presumption that one really has come to know that Q, for it suggests, though it does not strictly imply, that one has been in a good position to realize that Q, either relatively directly or on the basis of clues or reasons pointing to "Q."

This suggests why the discovery use of *learning that* seems to imply *knowing that* in the strong sense. Consider again our reporters, who learned (found out) after extensive investigation that the negotiations had been in progress for three weeks before the publicly announced agreement. The question "Granted they found out, but did they really know?" does not strike us as immediately relevant or natural. Those educators who stress so-called discovery and problem-solving methods in schooling may, in fact, be operating upon the general presumption that such methods lead to strong knowing as an outcome. And emphasis on *teaching*, with its distinctive connotations of rational explanation and critical dialogue, may have the same point: to develop a sort of learning in which the student will be capable of backing his beliefs by appropriate and sufficient means. To have learned that Q as a consequence of genuine teaching, given that "Q" is true, does seem to lend some weight to the presumption that one has come to know.

The notion of "teaching," unlike "learning," has, typically, *intentional* as well as *success* uses.[3] That is to say, teaching normally involves trying, whereas learning does not. To say of a child that he is learning to walk, that he is learning several new words every day, that he is learning how to conduct himself socially, that he is learning to express himself well in speech, does not in itself normally convey that he is *trying* to accomplish these things. It does not even convey that he is engaged or occupied in them, in the sense of thinking of what is going on, focusing his attention, and acting with care. Learning, it might thus be said, is not an *activity* but rather more nearly a *process*. We may surely distinguish the different stages of a process, and we may separate those situations in which the process has run its course to completion from those in which it has not. But such analyses do not presuppose either deliberateness or intention, although the latter *may*, in particular circumstances, be involved. We *can* try to learn this or that, but we often learn without trying at all; there is, moreover, no general presumption that any given case of learning is intentional.

Teaching appears quite different, by comparison. To say of someone that he is teaching conveys normally that he is engaged in an activity, rather than caught up in a process. It is to imply contextually that what he is doing is directed toward a goal and involves intention and care. He is, in short, trying, and what he is trying to bring about represents *success* in the activity, rather than simply the end-state of a process. We can, to be sure, speak of so-called "unintentional teaching," in which a person actually brings about a certain sort of learning, although without trying or even awareness on his part. But such reference will require that the word *teaching* be suitably qualified (e.g., by the word *unintentional*), or that supplementary explanation of the case be offered. Without such further information, a bare ascription of *teaching* contextually implies intention, whereas a success use of the verb (e.g., "Jones has taught his son how to swim") signifies intention brought to successful fruition. What does teaching have as its goal? What does a person engaged in teaching intend or try to bring about? Obviously, an appropriate bit of learning. In the particular case of *teaching that* with which we have so far been concerned, a person X teaching Y that Q, is trying to bring about Y's learning that Q. As we have seen, this involves Y's coming to accept "Q" or to believe that Q. If X has been successful in teaching Y that Q, Y has indeed learned that Q, has come to believe that Q.

The converse, of course, does not hold: One may learn that Q without having been taught it by anyone. Furthermore, we must not suppose that teaching can be *reduced to* trying to achieve someone's coming to believe something. One may try to propagate a belief in numerous ways other than teaching—for example, through deception, insinuation, advertising, hypnosis, propaganda, indoctrination, threats, bribery, and force. Nor must we be quick to identify teaching with schooling generally, for formal agencies of schooling have employed and often do employ methods other than teaching—for example, indoctrination, suggestion, threats, and force. Thus, if we think of *learning that* as referring to the acquisition of belief just in the context of schooling, we still cannot take teaching as simply directed toward learning as its goal, although teaching does have learning as its goal.

What distinguishes teaching, as we remarked earlier, is its special connection with rational explanation and critical dialogue: with the enterprise of giving honest reasons and welcoming radical questions. The person engaged in teaching does not merely want to bring about belief, but to bring it about through the exercise of free rational judgment by the student. This is what distinguishes teaching from propaganda or debating, for example. In teaching, the teacher is revealing his reasons for the beliefs he wants to transmit and is thus, in effect, submitting his own judgment to the critical scrutiny and evaluation of the student; he is fully engaged in the dialogue by which he hopes to teach, and is thus risking his own beliefs, in lesser or greater degree, as he teaches.

Teaching, it might be said, involves trying to bring about learning under severe restrictions of *manner*—that is to say, within the limitations imposed by the framework of rational discussion. Since teaching that Q presupposes that the teacher takes "Q" to be true (or at least within the legitimate range of truth approximation allowable for purposes of pedagogical simplification and facilitation) and since the activity of teaching appeals to the free rational judgment of the student, we might say that the teacher is trying to bring about knowledge, in the strong sense earlier discussed. For the presumption is that a person who is encouraged to form his beliefs through free rational methods is likely to be in a position to provide proper backing for them. The teacher does not strive merely to get the student to learn that Q, but also to get him to learn it in such a way as to know it—i.e., to be able to support it properly.

We must, however, admit that there will generally be differences of opinion as to the success or failure of the whole teaching operation. Cross-cultural cases provide the clearest illustrations. Consider the teacher of a distant age who strove to teach that evil spirits cause disease. He was (we have said) *trying* to get his students really to know this. Now we may admit that he was successful in getting them to believe that evil spirits cause disease and even in supporting this belief in a way that may have been reasonable in their cultural environment. We cannot, however, admit his *success* in getting his students to *know* that evil spirits cause disease, for *we* hold this doctrine to be false.

Is there not a difficulty here from the point of view of appraisal of teaching? We want to distinguish successful from unsuccessful teaching in this ancient era, but our present analysis forces us to judge all of it (at least with respect to such false doctrines as we have been considering) to have been uniformly unsuccessful. To meet this problem, we may propose a secondary or "subjective" notion of success to supplement the primary or "objective" notion we have been using. According to this secondary or subjective notion of success, we assume that the truth of the doctrine taught is to be judged from the teacher's point of view; we also judge the question of proper backing in a way that makes allowances for the prevalent standards and available data in the culture in question. Then we judge success in the normal manner. We can now make the wanted cross-cultural distinctions between successful and unsuccessful teaching even where, from an objective point of view and judged from our standpoint, it has been unsuccessful.

Any teaching is geared to what the teacher takes to be true, and his aim is not merely that his student learn what he takes to be true but that he be able to support it by criteria of proper backing taken to be authoritative. Insofar as the teacher is *teaching*, he is, in any event, risking his own particular truth judgments, for he is exposing them to the general critique of these criteria and to the free critical judgment of the student's mind.

One point of general importance should be especially noted. *Knowing that* attributions reflect the truth judgments and critical standards of the speaker; they commit him substantively to the beliefs he is assigning to others, and they hinge on the particular criteria of backing for beliefs, which he adopts. Thus, unlike attributions of *belief, learning that,* and *teaching that,* they reveal his own epistemological orientation to the items of belief in question; in this sense, they do more than merely describe the person to whom knowledge is being attributed.

We have, in sum, connected the educational ideas of learning and teaching with the cognitive ideas of knowledge and belief, as follows: Learning that Q involves coming to believe that Q. Under certain further conditions (truth of "Q" and, for the strong sense of *knowing,* proper backing of "Q"), it also involves coming to know that Q. Teaching that Q involves trying to bring about learning that (and belief that) Q, under characteristic restrictions of manner, and, furthermore, knowing that Q, as judged by the teacher from his own standpoint.

Now, there are certain classes of counterexamples that might be offered in opposition to these generalizations. A student might say, in reporting what he had learned on a certain day, "I learned that the gods dwelt on Olympus," or, if a student of philosophy, "I learned that the world of sense is an illusion." These reports might indeed be true, without the student's actually coming to *believe* that the gods dwelt on Olympus or that the world of sense is an illusion. Such reports are, however, plausibly interpreted as elliptical. What is really intended is, "I learned that it was believed (by the Greeks) that the gods dwelt on Olympus," or, "I learned that it was said (by such and such a philosopher) that the world of sense is an illusion."

Another sort of counterexample is provided by the case of X, who is teaching Y that metals expand when heated but who does not really care whether Y believes this or not. He is not trying to get Y to believe or to qualify (from his point of view) as knowing that metals expand when heated. He is only preparing Y to do what is necessary to pass the end-term examination. He may not even care about that; he may only be trying to get through the day. First, as to the latter case, it is quite possible for a *teacher* not to be engaged in *teaching* at a given time. To be called a teacher is, typically, to be described as having a certain institutional role in the process of schooling, rather than as engaging in teaching activity; we must avoid the assumption that whatever a teacher does on the job is properly describable as teaching. Secondly (as to the former case), we might well differentiate teaching *Y* that metals expand when heated from teaching *Y* how to handle examination questions relating to this subject in order to facilitate passing. It is, in fact, possible to do one of these without doing the other; from the time of the Sophists (at least), it has been recognized that teaching might be geared not toward knowledge of propositions taken as true but rather toward the acquisition of skills in handling the outward manifestations of such knowledge. There are analogous cases, moreover, where the latter aim is quite respectable—for example, where teaching is geared toward the development of skills in handling and applying theories rather than toward acceptance of these theories as true.[4]

RANGES OF COGNITIVE AND EDUCATIONAL TERMS

Our discussion of the previous section dealt with certain general connections between the educational terms *learning* and *teaching* and the cognitive terms *knowing* and *believing*. Our discussion was restricted, however, to comparable uses of these terms—i.e., *learning that, teaching that, knowing that,* and *believing that.* We must now turn to the question of their several ranges of use, which differ in important ways. We shall then have a clearer idea of the landscape within which our previous considerations may be located. Further, we shall find reason to avoid identifying the range of *education* with the range of *knowledge*. Following our exploration of the larger territory, we shall turn to detailed analyses of the region where educational and cognitive ranges overlap.

We may begin by suggesting that *know* is a term of wider range than *believe*. We can speak not only of *knowing that* but also of *knowing how to;* we can speak only of *believing that.* We may say not only "*X* knows that Napoleon was defeated at Waterloo" but also "*X* believes that Napoleon was defeated at Waterloo." However, though we may say "*X* knows how to ride a bicycle," we *cannot* say "*X* believes how to ride a bicycle." This fact may be conveniently formulated by labeling the *that* use *propositional* and the *how to* use *procedural*, and saying that whereas there is a propositional use of both *know* and *believe*, there is a procedural use only of *know*.

It must immediately be acknowledged, to be sure, that we have the construction *believing in* but not *knowing in. X* may be said to believe in God, in God's benevolence, in the future of the U.N., in democracy, or in John Jones. However, it seems possible to suggest plausible interpretations of *believing in* as propositional, in context: To believe in God is, in many typical contexts, for example, to believe that there is a God; to believe in God's benevolence is to believe that God is benevolent; to believe in the future of the U.N. is to believe that the U.N. has a future; to believe in democracy is to believe that democracy is good or that it has a future; to believe in Jones is to believe that Jones will satisfy the trust placed in him or the hopes for his good performance or achievement. There is, it would appear, no single formula of reduction for *believing in* statements; yet, with the help of contextual clues, it does seem plausible to suppose that reduction can be carried through along the lines just suggested, singly or in combination.

Assuming such reduction, belief will be construable as solely propositional, while knowing will clearly be not only propositional but also procedural. Nor is an extra procedural use the only prima facie indication of a wider range for *know* as contrasted with *believe*. We can speak, first of all, of knowing why there are tides but not of believing why there are tides, of knowing who committed the murder, or how or when it was committed, but not of believing who did it nor of believing how or when it was done. We can, to take a second set of examples, speak of knowing chess, music, or Scrabble but not of believing chess, music, or Scrabble. The first set of cases involves implicit reference to *questions* of one or another sort ("Why are there tides?" "Who committed the murder?" etc.); we will tag these as *question* uses. The second set we will label as *subject* uses, since they refer to the "subjects" chess, music, etc.

It is true that for some subjects we can also apply *belief* notions. For example, we can speak not only of knowing the theory of evolution but of believing the theory of evolution. Nonetheless, we cannot apply *belief* notions analogously throughout the whole category of knowable subjects—e.g., to chess or music.

Moreover, even in cases of subjects where *belief* does apply, it is propositional where the corresponding knowing is *not;* it is, furthermore, not implied by (nor included in) the corresponding *knowing*, as is the case with propositional uses. That is to say, *knowing that* metals expand when heated implies *believing that* metals expand when heated, but knowing the theory of evolution does not imply believing the theory of evolution. To say that someone believes the theory of evolution is to say he accepts it or takes it as true. To say he knows it is, normally, to say not *more* than this but something *different:* it is to say rather that he is acquainted with this theory or that he can recognize, handle, and perhaps state it. To *believe* a theory is, in short, to believe *that* it is correct or true; to *know* a theory is *not* to know *that* it is correct or true. The relevant sense of *know* is different from that of the *propositional* use we have discussed.

Now it may, in fact, be suggested that subject and question uses of *know* are reducible to procedural ones: To *know a theory* is to *know how to* formulate and possibly work with it; to *know why* there are tides is to *know how to* answer correctly the question why there are tides. Alternatively one might propose to reduce question uses, at least, to propositional ones, taking "*X* knows who the murderer is" as "There is a true answer to the question 'Who is the murderer?' and *X* knows that this answer is true." These suggestions may be thought plausible or they may not, but we need not decide whether they are adequate, at least for our present purposes. It is sufficient if we recognize that belief may be interpreted as, in any event, propositional. On the other hand, knowing is not always propositional; it is not always, nor always reducible to, *knowing that.* Even if the above mentioned reductions were to be carried out, we should still be left with a procedural as well as a propositional use of *know.* Nor could it be plausibly proposed to reduce the procedural use itself to the propositional: To what *knowing that* expression would "knowing how to type" correspond?

The range of *knowing* may thus be said to be larger than that of *believing.* If we now turn to the terms *learning* and *teaching,* we find that they are applicable in all the cases so far discussed; they are not limited to simply propositional uses. The student may learn or be taught that Napoleon was defeated at Waterloo. He may learn or be taught how to ride a bicycle or how to type. He may learn or be taught why there are tides. He may learn or be taught chess or the theory of evolution. Since, however, the notion of belief is not applicable in any but the first and the last of these cases (i.e., believing that Napoleon was defeated at Waterloo, believing the theory of evolution), it cannot be generally tied to learning and teaching as it was in the specifically propositional cases earlier discussed. Taking learning first, we cannot say, for example, that if *X* has learned how to type, he has come to believe how to type, as we *can* say that if he has learned that Napoleon was defeated at Waterloo, he has come to believe it. We cannot say that if *X* has learned why there are tides, he has come to believe why there are tides. Nor can we say he has come to believe chess if he has learned chess. Rather, we need to say that if he has learned how to type, he has come to know how to type; if he has learned why there are tides, he has come to know why there are tides; if he has learned chess, he has come to know chess. Moreover, even though it *is* possible to speak of believing the theory of evolution, as it is not possible to speak of believing chess, it is false to say that if *X* has learned the theory, he has come to believe it; we should rather say he has come to know the theory—which, as we have seen, is a different thing from coming to accept the theory as true.

Analogously, we cannot introduce belief into our general account of teaching as we did earlier. For example, we cannot say that, in teaching Y how to type, the teacher is trying to bring about Y's believing how to type. Rather, we need to say he is trying to get Y to know how to type. Similarly, he wants the student to know the theory of evolution, or chess, or why there are tides.

The main result to be noted is that, while the range of *knowing* is larger than that of *belief*, *learning* and *teaching* are at least as large in range as *knowing*. Education outstrips belief in its range, we might say, concerned as it also is with the development of skills, procedural techniques, subject familiarity—in short, with everything that might be characterized in terms of knowing. Nonetheless, we must not suppose that the range of education coincides with that of knowing. In fact, it goes beyond it; the concepts of learning and teaching are applicable in cases where *knowing* is not.

This point may be introduced by the consideration that *learning to* and *teaching to* have no counterparts such as *believing to* or *knowing to*. The child, for example, may *learn to* be punctual or be *taught to* be punctual, but he cannot then be said to *believe* or *know to* be punctual. His learning here is best thought of not in terms of knowledge but rather in terms of active propensities, tendencies, or habits of conduct. He has not necessarily nor simply come to believe something new, nor has he simply or necessarily achieved a new procedural facility or a new subject familiarity. He has, rather, acquired a new trait or pattern of action. His conduct now, though not before, is characterizable as generally displaying punctuality.

The *learning to* and *teaching to* expressions are, furthermore, not limited to the case of active propensities; they extend also to other cases, which are difficult to classify but which might perhaps be here labeled *attainments:* The child might, for instance, learn to *appreciate* music or to *understand* the relation between multiplication and addition, but he could not be said to *believe* or to *know to* appreciate or understand. So in respect of attainments as well as propensities our educational terms outstrip *knowing* in range.

But perhaps to understand something is reducible to knowing it, so learning to understand X is learning to know X. While, however, there may indeed be contexts in which knowing X conveys the connotation of understanding X, it does not seem plausible to make the proposed *general* reduction. A person may say without contradiction, "I know the doctrines of the existentialists, but I don't understand them." Or we may say of a child, "He knows Newton's laws (or Shakespeare's plays) but doesn't yet understand them." The limits of such knowing are perhaps elastic, involving at times familiarity, recognition, acquaintance, and ability to formulate, paraphrase, and use but not in every case including understanding. What constitutes understanding if it is not simply familiarity or skill of a certain sort is a separate question. Some have suggested that understanding involves something analogous to perception: seeing the point. Or it might be construed to include having explained or paraphrased the doctrine in question in special terms, initially intelligible to the person. Or, again, it might be thought to require a certain degree of experience or maturity (as in understanding Shakespeare's plays). However we interpret it, it seems *not* to reduce to the subject use of *know*.

It might now be suggested that, although there are no *believing to* or *knowing to* locutions, a certain kind of *believing that* or *knowing that* accompanies *learning to*. The idea, in effect, may be to reduce the latter to *learning that:* The child who has learned *to* be punctual has come to believe or know *that he ought to* be punctual; the child who has learned to appreciate music has come to believe or know that he ought to appreciate music; having learned to understand multiplication, he has come to know that he ought to understand multiplication.

This suggestion does not, however, seem to be tenable. Certainly the converses fail even though in some contexts we interpret, for example, the child's knowing that he ought to be punctual as implying that he is punctual. But even the inferences from *learning to* statements to the proposed *believing that* or *knowing that* statements break down. A boy may learn to bite his nails or to smoke without coming to believe or to know that he ought to bite his nails or to smoke. A person may come to appreciate a painting or to understand the concepts of atomic theory without holding that he ought to; indeed, the question may be raised whether it can meaningfully be said that one ought to appreciate or understand, as distinct from trying to appreciate or understand. Nor, in coming to appreciate a painting, does a person always come to believe that it is a *good* painting; and surely the converse here fails also. (Appreciation may, to be sure, involve liking, but liking is itself not reducible to a belief in the goodness of the object.)

Finally, it might be suggested that *learning to* is really *procedural,* a matter of acquiring more or less complex skills or techniques, describable in terms of *knowing how*. There are some examples in which this suggestion seems to find a plausible interpretation: To say that someone has learned to swim or to drive a car is indeed to say that he has come to know how to swim or to drive—he has acquired swimming or driving skills. These are, however, cases in which the *learning to* expression could well be supplanted by *learning how to:* To have learned to swim or to drive is to have learned how to swim or to drive. Not every case of *learning to* can, however, be thus rewritten in terms of *learning how to,* nor can it be interpreted as a matter of acquiring some relevant bit of know-how. To learn to be a good neighbor or citizen is not the same as learning how to be a good neighbor or citizen. To learn to pay one's debts is not the same as learning how to pay one's debts; it is not, for example, simply the sort of thing that is involved in learning the proper use of a checkbook.[5] Learning various techniques for ensuring one's punctuality is not yet learning to be punctual. To acquire a skill is one thing, to acquire a habit or propensity quite another. The case seems even stronger with respect to what we have called *attainments*. For, whereas active propensities often have strictly associated techniques (e.g., a person who enjoys swimming and swims regularly knows how to swim), attainments do not have strictly associated techniques. A person who appreciates music is not properly said to know how to appreciate music; one who understands quantum theory is not well described as knowing how to understand quantum theory. (It would certainly seem strange if someone said that he knew very well *how* to appreciate music but didn't choose to, or that he knew *how* to understand quantum theory but hadn't in fact understood it lately.) Certainly there are techniques *embedded* in attainments: One who understands quantum theory knows how to read, and one who appreciates music knows how to listen. But these bits of know-how are not strictly associated; they are not equivalent to knowing how to *understand,* and knowing how to *appreciate,* respectively. Understanding and appreciation cannot, it would seem, readily be said to be exercises of technique or know-how, as swimming might be said to be an exercise of swimming know-how. For there seems to be no such thing as an *understanding know-how* or an *appreciating know-how.* Much less can learning to understand or to appreciate be suggested to reduce to mere acquisition of such know-how.

Skills, or procedures and elements of know-how, carry with them a cluster of associated notions that do not all apply *either* in the case of propensities *or* in the case of attainments. First of all, a skill or element of know-how, once acquired, may or may not be exercised, given the relevant opportunities; a person may be said to have a skill or the relevant know-how even though he never (or very rarely) exercises it after having acquired it, although he has ample opportunity to do so. There are many people who have learned and who know how to swim but who do not any longer swim at all, or only very rarely, though they have the chance. We may conjecture that their technique is rusty, but we do not feel compelled to deny that they *can* swim. By contrast, a person who has the habit or trait of punctuality is a person who *is* generally punctual on relevant occasions. If a person who had been punctual began to show up late for all, or nearly all, of his appointments and continued thus consistently for an appreciable length of time, we should wish to say he had lost the habit of punctuality. A person could not claim still to be punctual on the grounds that he had once been, though for a long time he had never, or hardly ever, arrived anywhere on time. In short, it is quite possible to say that X knows how to swim but never does; it would, however, strike us as self-contradictory to say that X has the habit of punctuality but never shows up on time. For attainments, the very notion of repeated performance is suspect: We may speak of one who knows how to swim as swimming every Tuesday, of a punctual student as showing up on time to class twenty times in a row. But what would it mean to say of a person who understands the quantum theory that he had understood it every Tuesday last month, or of a person who appreciates modern art that he had appreciated it twenty times in a row?

Secondly, in the case of skill or know-how a person may clearly decide not to exercise it. There is nothing puzzling in saying that a man knows how to play tennis but chooses not to. An analogous description is indeed possible also for habits, for a man may deliberately control his own propensities on particular occasions; a smoker may decide not to smoke now, for example. There seems, however, to be no such analogue for attainments: A person with an understanding of quantum theory cannot choose not to understand it; one who appreciates poetry cannot decide not to appreciate poetry on Mondays. Even for habits, moreover, the analogy is limited; where control goes far enough, it turns into elimination of the habit in question.

Thirdly, the notion of practice seems clearly relevant to skills and know-how; they are, indeed, typically built up through repeated trials or performances. Analogously, we may speak of habits, too, as being formed through repeated trials; through smoking again and again one may, for example, develop a genuine smoking habit. A parallel description seems, however, out of the question in the case of attainments. One cannot develop an understanding of the quantum theory by understanding it over and over again, nor can one strengthen or deepen one's understanding by repeated performances of understanding; the very notion of repeated performances is here suspect, as argued above. It makes sense to tell a student to practice playing a certain piece of music; it makes no sense to tell him to practice appreciating what he plays.

Finally, the notions of proficiency or mastery seem peculiarly applicable to skills. One may attain proficiency in driving or become a master in chess, but one cannot well be described as proficient in punctuality or honesty nor as having become a master of the habit of taking a walk before breakfast. Neither can one be said to be proficient in understanding a theory nor to have mastered the appreciation of Bach. A person may have more or less understanding of a topic, he may appreciate a poem less or more, but he cannot be called a good understander or appreciator as he might be called a good driver, typist, or chess-player. Similarly, a person's habit of smoking or of fingernail-biting may be weak or strong, deeply or less deeply ingrained, easy or difficult to break, but he cannot well be described as a good smoker or fingernail-biter.

The upshot is that neither propensities nor attainments can well be assimilated to the category of skills or know-how, nor can *learning to* and *teaching to* be construed as really procedural. It follows that the range of educational concepts is not only larger than that of belief, as we saw earlier; it is also larger than that of knowing. Education outstrips cognitive notions altogether in its range, embracing, as we have seen, also the formation of propensities and traits, and the development of understanding and appreciation.

ILLUSTRATIVE DEFINITION OF PROPOSITIONAL KNOWLEDGE

Having seen the wide range of educational notions, we now turn to a consideration of that part of the range which overlaps the range of *knowing*. The case of knowing that has figured most prominently in classical discussions in epistemology is the propositional case, and to this we address ourselves first. We shall find it convenient to introduce here a sample definition of *knowing that* as an anchor for our future discussions of the propositional case. This definition sets three conditions for *knowing that,* and we shall refer to these as the *belief* condition, the *evidence* condition, and the *truth* condition.[6]

X knows that Q

if and only if

> (i) X believes that Q,
> (ii) X has adequate evidence that Q,
> and   (iii) Q.

This definition takes all three stated conditions as jointly defining *knowing that* and thus corresponds to the "strong sense" of *know* discussed early in the first section of the present chapter. The "weak sense" is easily gotten by simply omitting condition (ii). In each of the following three chapters we shall take one of the above conditions and discuss certain outstanding issues relating to its interpretation. We turn first to truth.

•

CHAPTER TWO

Knowledge and Truth

•

THE TRUTH CONDITION OF PROPOSITIONAL KNOWLEDGE

At the end of the last chapter, we referred to the third condition of our definition as a *truth condition*. The point is that when we *assert* that a person X knows that Q, we are not only (in effect) affirming the truth of our whole assertion, but we are committing ourselves also to the truth of the embedded substantive statement, "Q." We may, of course, be mistaken in both claims, for it may, in fact, be the case neither that X knows that Q, nor that Q. We might also be mistaken in just one of these claims, for X may, in fact, *not* know that Q, even though the statement "Q" is true. But what is ruled out by the truth condition is the remaining possibility: that we are right in holding X to know that Q but mistaken about the truth of "Q." The truth condition thus is to be understood as asserting: *If* it is true that X knows that Q, *then* it is true that Q. Further, the notion of *truth* in the foregoing exposition is only a convenience; the content of the relevant assertion can, for example, also be put as follows: If X knows that Q, then Q (no matter what statement is put in place of both occurrences of "Q"). The important point in any event is that in asserting, or taking it as true, that X knows that Q, we are committed also to asserting, or taking it as true, that Q, for the latter is a "necessary condition" of the former.

To say we are committed to asserting that Q, does not of course mean that we need to have this commitment in the forefront of our consciousness whenever we judge X to know that Q. The truth condition does not reflect what goes on in the consciousness of the person attributing knowledge; rather, it purports to reflect an objective commitment of such attribution, evidenced indirectly in the way specific attributes are critically evaluated: In particular, a knowledge attribution will be withdrawn or rejected if it is denied that *Q*. We discussed a relevant example in the first section of Chapter I. The student claiming to know that evil spirits cause disease will not be acknowledged by us to know any such thing, for we deny that evil spirits do cause disease. We may, however, if we accept the sincerity of the claim, admit that this student *believes* that evil spirits cause disease, though he believes it mistakenly. If you were to hear me say I knew the play would begin at eight o'clock, and you had just been informed by the box office that it would start at eight-thirty, you would suppose me to be mistaken in my belief. You would surely not describe me as *knowing* that the play would begin at eight, if you accepted the official word of the box office.

In general, if you think I am mistaken in my belief, you will deny that I know, no matter how sincere you judge me to be and no matter how strong you consider my conviction. For *X* to be judged mistaken is sufficient basis for rejecting the claim that he knows. It follows that if *X* is admitted to know, he must be judged not to be mistaken, and this is the point of the truth condition.

Additional grounds for this condition may be found in our common forms of speech. Whereas we may describe someone as mistakenly believing that whales are fish, we could not well describe him as mistakenly knowing that whales are fish. We may say a person is wrong in believing that water contracts upon freezing, but we would not say he is wrong in knowing that water contracts upon freezing. I don't contradict myself in saying, "Most people believe it's hard to learn symbolic logic, but they're wrong." I do, in contrast, seem clearly to contradict myself in saying, "Most people know it's hard to learn symbolic logic, but they're wrong." I may once have said, "I know I will never learn to type." Having learned, I do not say, "I once knew I would never learn to type, but I was wrong"; I say, rather, "I once believed I would never learn to type, but I was wrong." Having come to the realization that I was wrong, I withdraw the claim to have known. Finally, I may well say, "I believe that man's name is Jones, but I may be mistaken"; I cannot well say, "I know that man's name is Jones, but I may be mistaken."

Knowing, it would appear, is incompatible with being wrong or mistaken, and when I describe someone as knowing, I commit myself to his not being mistaken. In discussing other people's opinions, I may thus reveal my own by use of the word *know*, rather than concealing them by use of the word *believe*. If, for example, I say, "Plato believes there are ideal forms," you may well ask if I agree with him. If, by contrast, I say, "Dewey knows that inquiry arises out of problems," I have already indicated I agree with him.

We must now, however, recognize certain apparent counterexamples to the truth condition. Earlier, we saw that the student who said, "I learned that the gods dwelt on Olympus" could be taken as saying, "I learned that it was *believed* that the gods dwelt on Olympus." Now this same student, having done well in his examination, might be described by his teacher as *knowing* that the gods dwelt on Olympus, without any commitment on the teacher's part to assert that the gods did dwell on Olympus. The truth condition would, in such a case, be violated. The teacher's description might, however, also plausibly be interpreted as elliptical, the student being said to know *it was believed that* the gods dwelt on Olympus. Given such an interpretation, the truth condition would again be preserved, for the teacher *is* committed to the assertion that it was *believed* the gods dwelt on Olympus.

A somewhat analogous treatment accounts for the apparent counterexample, "John knows that Hamlet was a prince of Denmark," which may be taken as "John knows that Shakespeare's play asserts Hamlet to be a prince of Denmark." Here, too, the truth condition is preserved by spelling out the supposed content of knowledge, "knowing that" being understood, in effect, as "knowing it to be asserted that."

Another sort of apparent counterexample to the truth condition is presented by our description, not of the student, but of the Greeks themselves, in the sentence "The Greeks knew the gods dwelt on Olympus." Here the previous remedy fails, for we clearly do *not* mean that the Greeks *knew it was believed that* the gods dwelt on Olympus. What is intended here is rather that they *believed they knew that* the gods dwelt on Olympus, or that they were sure the gods dwelt on Olympus. The point is often expressed in such a formula as: "For the Greeks, the gods dwelt on Olympus." Under such interpretation, the truth condition is again preserved, for it applies only to knowing, not to *belief in* knowing.

Aside from apparent exceptions of the sorts we have just considered, which may be explained away by appropriately expanded expressions, we may take the truth condition as holding directly: The statement "X knows that Q" commits the speaker to the assertion represented by "Q." If he says, "X mistakenly believes that Q," he commits himself, on the other hand, to the denial of "Q." He remains neutral as between "Q" and "not-Q" if he merely says, "X believes that Q." Further, if he denies rather than attributes knowledge, he also retains his neutrality. For example, "He does not know that the car is in the garage" implies neither that it is nor that it is not. It may be that the car *is* in the garage, and to deny that *he* knows is to say that he does not think it is, or is not in a position to be sure that it is. Or, it may be that the car is *not* in the garage, and to deny that he knows is to say simply that he does not, because he cannot, know what is not the case.

KNOWING AS AN ACHIEVEMENT

The truth condition suggests that knowledge attributions have a double function which may be characterized as follows: In attributing knowledge to X, I not only describe X but say something about the world. I characterize his state of mind in terms of *belief that* such and such is the case, and I further add that such and such *is* the case. These two component assertions are logically independent. Certainly, we cannot generally *assume* that if X believes that Q, then Q, nor vice versa. The category of *mistake* is surely applicable to belief in just such cases in which the belief content "Q" is negated by the actual fact that not-Q.

Belief descriptions of X are descriptions with embedded, though unasserted, substantive sentences—i.e., those represented by "Q." A person may, for instance, be described as believing that the world is flat; his state of mind has here been characterized by means of the embedded sentence, "The world is flat," though this sentence is surely *not* asserted by the belief description itself. We can, however, independently raise the question whether or not the world *is* flat— that is, whether or not the facts are such as to render the embedded belief-content sentence true. If the answer is no, the belief is mistaken; otherwise, not. To say, "X *knows* that Q" is then to affirm not merely that X believes that Q, but also that "Q" is independently true, that X's belief is, as a matter of fact, not mistaken. Knowing is thus incompatible with mistake. If "Q" is, in fact, false, then X's sincerity and strength of conviction may be as great as you like, but he does not *know* that Q, for such knowing requires not only the proper state of X's mind but the proper state of the world. One might say, not too misleadingly, that *believing* aims at the truth while *knowing that* succeeds in this aim.

Another way of putting the matter is to say (perhaps more misleadingly) that whereas *believing that* has a purely psychological reference, requiring only some appropriate state of mind, *knowing that* does not, in general, have purely psychological reference, for it also makes independent reference to an appropriate state of the world. Unlike the traditional view that knowing and believing are related forms of mental activity, the present idea leads us to differentiate sharply between them, in denying that knowing is simply a mental or psychological affair.

Many modern writers have defended this thesis from differing standpoints and have brought various auxiliary considerations in its support. R. M. Chisholm, for example, writes, "We must not think of knowing as being, in any sense, a 'species of' believing or accepting. A man can be said to believe firmly, or reluctantly, or hesitatingly, but no one can be said to *know* firmly, or reluctantly, or hesitatingly."[1] J. L. Austin, in a widely quoted passage, stresses the oddness of classifying knowing and believing as cognitive acts along the same continuum: "Saying 'I know,'" he writes, "is *not* saying 'I have performed a specially striking feat of cognition, superior, in the same scale as believing and being sure, even to being merely quite sure': for there *is* nothing in that scale superior to being quite sure."[2] Austin also points to differences in the way first-person assertions of belief and of knowledge are challenged. We ask, "*How* do you know?" and "*Why* do you believe?" but not vice versa. "And in this . . . not merely such other words as 'suppose', 'assume', etc., but also the expressions 'be sure' and 'be certain', follow the example of 'believe', not that of 'know'" (p. 46). Furthermore, as Austin notes, a challenge that is unsuccessfully met is treated quite differently in the case of knowledge and in the case of belief. If the *belief* challenge is not met to the satisfaction of the challenger, he will say "something such as 'That's very poor evidence to go on: you oughtn't to believe it on the strength of that alone'" (p. 46). On the other hand, if the *knowledge* challenge is not properly met, the answer will be "something such as 'Then you *don't* know any such thing', or 'But that doesn't prove it: in that case you don't really know it at all.' . . . The 'existence' of your alleged belief is not challenged, but the 'existence' of your alleged knowledge *is* challenged. If we like to say that 'I believe', and likewise 'I am sure' and 'I am certain', are descriptions of subjective mental or cognitive states or attitudes, or what not, then 'I know' is not that, or at least not merely that: it functions differently in talking" (pp. 46–47).

In denying that there is sufficient reason to hold that your belief is correct, or that it squares with the facts, I conclude only that your belief is not well-grounded, not that it does not exist. To find good reason to say it does not exist is, of course, theoretically possible: I should need to find appropriate indications about your "internal" or psychological state, however. For example, I might have adequate indication to suppose that, in making your belief statement, you were insincere, lying, joking, or fooling yourself. In any event, I could not rely merely on showing your belief to be factually wrong. By contrast, in the case of knowing, without having any comparable indication about your "internal" or psychological state, and merely by showing cause to hold your knowledge claim untrue to the facts, I am able to conclude that you *do not* know. The conclusion seems to be that knowing, unlike believing, has independent factual reference. The truth condition, which makes explicit this factual reference, thus seems to rule out the traditional (and still current) notion that knowing is simply and purely a cognitive task, faculty, activity, state, process, or performance.

That knowing is an achievement and, in particular, not a kind of mental performance or activity has been argued by Gilbert Ryle.[3]

Ryle begins by introducing the general notion of a *category-mistake*, which he illustrates as follows: A visitor to Oxford or Cambridge is shown various colleges, libraries, offices, museums, etc., and then he asks "Where is the University?" mistakenly assigning the University to the same category as the things he has already been shown. Ryle offers no definition of what he intends by *category*, but his guiding idea seems to be that members of the same category should be subject to *the same sorts* of qualification, and accessible to *the same sorts* of question. The urgent theoretical problem for any definition of *category* is to say what is meant by *the same sorts* in each case, but let us here waive this problem and follow Ryle in using our unanalyzed, intuitive notions of relevant sameness.

If we do so, it appears plausible that knowing does belong in a different category from activities or performances. For example, to the question, "What are you doing?" one might answer, "Reading a book," "Eating dinner," "Studying my notes," "Listening to the radio." But one could not well answer, "Knowing that 2 and 7 are 9." If you ask someone to go for a walk, he might say, "I'm too busy studying to join you," or "I'd rather study," or "I'm occupied in studying," but he could not very well say, "I'm too busy knowing," or "I'd rather know than come for a walk," or "I'm occupied in knowing something at the moment." In general, one can say, "I am swimming," or "I am reading," or "I am typing," but not "I am knowing." A person may read quickly or slowly, carefully or carelessly, attentively or distractedly, but he cannot know either slowly or quickly, carefully or carelessly, attentively or distractedly.

Performances are well or ill done and subject, as a rule, to qualification by the adjectives *competent, good,* or *skilled*. A person may be said to be a competent typist, a good dancer, a skilled mechanic, but neither a competent, nor a good, nor a skilled knower. A performance or activity may be interrupted: A telephone call may, for example, interrupt someone while he is reading a book and prevent him from finishing it; no student can, however, claim that he had been similarly interrupted in the course of knowing that Napoleon was defeated at Waterloo and had been prevented from completing the job. Performances can generally be improved through practice, but one cannot practice knowing that 7 and 6 are 13. One can decide whether or not to perform, if one knows how; one cannot analogously be described as deciding whether or not to know that 7 and 6 are 13, if one knows how to know this. As in the case of understanding and appreciation discussed earlier (in the second section of Chapter I), knowing does not seem to fit performance, activity, or skill categories at all, nor does it belong with propensities, for which the notions of decision and repeated trial are also relevant. Knowing appears to resemble rather those things that fit the categories of attainment, attitude, or, most broadly, *state.* In particular, it would seem to be a "category-mistake" to talk of knowing as a task, activity, or performance.

Now the very same conclusion will be seen to apply also to believing, for in every one of the examples considered in the last two paragraphs, believing behaves in just the same way as knowing. Thus, if knowing is not a performance, neither is believing. We shall discuss believing in detail in Chapter IV, but one point seems now evident. While believing may be construed as a *purely psychological* state without any special difficulty, this seems ruled out in the case of knowing, for knowing-attributions assert not only the existence of a relevant psychological state, but also the existence of some appropriate, generally independent, state of the world. Knowing-descriptions, in fact, attribute belief states, but they also assert the embedded sentences by means of which such belief states are identified. Such assertion in effect proclaims the attributed belief states to be successful by a logically independent criterion.

In the light of analogous considerations, Ryle treats knowing as an *achievement,* and places it within a general category with comparable characteristics. He is not so much concerned to contrast knowing with believing, however, as to contrast knowing with the following of certain procedures of inquiry. Inquiry is a matter of our efforts to attain knowledge, whereas knowledge requires the satisfaction of independent conditions holding as a matter of fact. Though knowing that always presupposes believing that, it does not, presumably, always presuppose the following of relevant procedures; Ryle himself indicates that there are such things as "lucky achievements" (p. 151). Knowing that may nonetheless be represented as an achievement, of which inquiring is the "subservient task activity." Ryle's main concern, as we shall see presently, is to undercut the epistemological doctrine of infallibility: Knowing, as an achievement, cannot fail, but this is not to say there is some inquiry procedure which cannot fail. We shall deal with this line of argument in the next section, addressing ourselves now to Ryle's concept of achievements.

Many of the verbs we use to describe performance

> signify the occurrence not just of actions but of suitable actions. They signify achievements. Verbs like "spell", "catch", "solve", "find", "win", "cure", "score", "deceive", "persuade", "arrive" and countless others signify not merely that some performance has been gone through, but also that something has been brought off by the agent going through it. They are verbs of success (p. 130).

Achievement verbs are quite different, says Ryle, from activity or process verbs; in particular they are different from corresponding task verbs, and to assimilate the two classes is a confusion of categories.

One big difference between the logical force of a task verb and that of a corresponding achievement verb is that in applying an achievement verb we are asserting that some state of affairs obtains over and above that which consists in the performance, if any, of the subservient task activity. For a runner to win, not only must he run but also his rivals must be at the tape later than he; for a doctor to effect a cure, his patient must both be treated and be well again; for the searcher to find the thimble, there must be a thimble in the place he indicates at the moment when he indicates it; and for the mathematician to prove a theorem, the theorem must be true and follow from the premises from which he tries to show that it follows (150).

When a person is described as having fought and won, or as having journeyed and arrived, he is not being said to have done two things, but to have done one thing with a certain upshot. Similarly a person who has aimed and missed has not followed up one occupation by another; he has done one thing, which was a failure. So, while we expect a person who has been trying to achieve something to be able to say without research what he has been engaged in, we do not expect him necessarily to be able to say without research whether he has achieved it. Achievements and failures are not occurrences of the right type to be objects of what is often, if misleadingly, called "immediate awareness". They are not acts, exertions, operations or performances, but, with reservations for purely lucky achievements, the fact that certain acts, operations, exertions or performances have had certain results (pp. 150–151).

AVOIDING THE BELIEF IN CERTAINTY

Ryle suggests that one consequence of assimilating achievements to tasks is a mistaken belief in *infallibility,* in a mental faculty or performance immune from error. Thus, to separate achievements from tasks is not only to avoid a serious category-mistake but to undercut one likely source of the traditional notion that knowing implies not only truth but also *certainty.* Let us turn first to a rationalistic source of this notion, associated with the idea of necessary truth.

We noted earlier (in the second section of the Introduction) the rationalistic appeal to mathematics as an educational ideal. The attractiveness of this ideal lies in its link with necessity, based on the notion that mathematical truths not only tell us what *is* the case but also what *could not possibly* be otherwise. Given such a conception, if one knows a mathematical truth, then he not only *is not* wrong but *could not* be wrong, in the special sense that what is known is necessary. It may seem only a short step to the idea that if one knows *anything*, he *could not* be wrong, in the sense that his knowing consists in the exercise of an infallible mental faculty, an error-free intuition. From the notion of a necessary or certain *object of* knowledge, one comes thus to the idea of a certain—that is, infallible—*cognitive performance or faculty*. These two notions are, however, logically independent, and it is a fallacy to infer the one from the other. Putting the matter in other words, it might be said that a person who knows that 2 and 2 are 4 could not be wrong, in the sense that he would still be right *on this score* no matter how the world might change. It would be a totally different thing to say that he could not be wrong, in the sense that he would still be right no matter what other proposition he were to intuit or apprehend in psychologically similar manner, such manner being definitive of knowing.

Though it is clearly a fallacy to pass from the certainty of an *object of knowledge* to the certainty of a *cognitive faculty or performance*, taken to be constitutive of knowing, the latter notion may of course be bolstered in other ways. One of these ways depends on the truth condition. For, as we noted earlier, the truth condition has the force of denying that knowing is compatible with being mistaken. If anyone *knows* that such and such is the case, he is always in fact *correct* in that such and such *is* the case, no matter what "such and such" stands for. He cannot at one and the same time know *and* be wrong or mistaken, with respect to the same proposition. If a person knows that 2 and 2 are 4, the truth condition itself assures us that he would still be right no matter what other proposition he were to *know*. If knowing is now construed as a mental performance or task of some special sort, it follows that, since it is *never* mistaken, it is always right, therefore certain. Knowing is, thus, the exercise of an infallible mental faculty or capacity or the performance of a special mental task which is guaranteed to be successful. If only we perform mentally in the requisite manner, we are certain of attaining the truth.

The notion of an infallible mental performance has here been gotten from the truth condition *plus* the construal of knowing as a mental performance. The trouble is, as Ryle argues, that knowing is not a performance at all, and so cannot be an infallible performance. Knowing is, rather, an achievement. To say, however, that all *achievements* are successful is trivial; in particular, it does not at all imply that there is some *mode of performance* which is immune to failure. To distinguish clearly between achievements and performances is thus to eliminate a further source of the belief that knowing implies infallibility or certainty. Ryle, in the following passage, makes this point not only with respect to knowing but also with respect to other epistemological achievement words.

The distinction between task verbs and achievement verbs or "try" verbs and "got it" verbs frees us from another theoretical nuisance. It has long been realized that verbs like "know", "discover", "solve", "prove", "perceive", "see", and "observe" (at least in certain standard uses of "observe") are in an important way incapable of being qualified by adverbs like "erroneously" and "incorrectly". Automatically construing these and kindred verbs as standing for special kinds of operations or experiences, some epistemologists have felt themselves obliged to postulate that people possess certain special inquiry procedures in following which they are subject to no risk of error. They need not, indeed they cannot, execute them carefully, for they provide no scope for care. The logical impossibility of a discovery being fruitless, or of a proof being invalid, has been misconstrued as a quasi-causal impossibility of going astray. If only the proper road were followed, or if only the proper faculty were given its head, incorrigible observations or self-evident intuitions could not help ensuing. So men are sometimes infallible. Similarly if hitting the bull's eye were construed as a special kind of aiming, or if curing were construed as a special kind of treatment, then, since neither could, in logic, be at fault, it would follow that there existed special fault-proof ways of aiming and doctoring. There would exist some temporarily infallible marksmen and some occasionally infallible doctors (pp. 152–153).

As Ryle sums it up in another passage,

Simple logic "prevents" curing, finding, solving, and hitting the bull's eye from being bungled or unavailing. The fact that doctors cannot cure unsuccessfully does not mean that they are infallible doctors; it only means that there is a contradiction in saying that a treatment which has succeeded has not succeeded (p. 238).

The particular application of Ryle's argument to the case of knowing seems clear enough. Knowing is not a strategy of inquiry any more than curing is a strategy of treatment. The fact that if you know, you are not mistaken is thus no more reason to suppose there is some infallible investigative procedure than the fact that if you cure the patient, he recovers is a reason to suppose there is some medical strategy which never fails.

It is, nonetheless, difficult to understand the *general* contrast between tasks and achievements, as presented by Ryle. Does he mean only that certain pairs of verbs are recognizably related as achievement verb to corresponding task verb, in the way, for example, that *cure* is related to *treat*? But he includes among achievement verbs such words as *spell* and *persuade*, which seem to lack corresponding task verbs, although there are, to be sure, the constructions *try to spell* and *try to persuade*, which seem intuitively to denote relevant "subservient tasks." On the other hand, if we allow the latter to serve as task expressions corresponding, respectively, to the achievement verbs *spell* and *persuade*, we must allow also, for example, *try to walk* and *try to run*—whereupon *walk* and *run* also turn out to be achievement verbs, rather than task, performance, or activity verbs, as we should intuitively judge them to be. Indeed, it is hard to see how we could prevent performances generally from turning into achievements once we allowed *try* constructions: Not only would winning be an achievement, but running would also be an achievement; surely, running involves some state of affairs over and above the "subservient task" of trying to run. The notion, in short, of two exclusive categories of tasks and achievements would collapse.

Is perhaps the essential point of distinction rather that some verbs can, while others cannot, be appropriately qualified by notions of success? We can, for instance, speak of treating the patient successfully or unsuccessfully but not of curing the patient successfully or unsuccessfully. And while we do not normally use the expression "running a race successfully (or unsuccessfully)," we may intelligibly ask of a runner in a race whether he has won, recognizing that winning is the implicit goal for which he has striven in running, the relevant form of success toward which his running has been directed; we cannot, by contrast, ask a similar question of the winner, for winning is not in the same way directed toward some implicit goal.

This idea seems plausible, but though it does not generally turn performances into achievements, as with the previous proposal, it does nevertheless give us an unduly expanded category of achievements. For example, walking would turn out an achievement, since we neither speak of walking successfully or unsuccessfully, nor do we conceive of walking as embodying a striving toward some implicit goal. By analogous reasoning, sitting, standing, and sleeping would turn out to be achievements, in a class with finding, winning, and arriving. It might be suggested that finding, winning, and arriving normally convey an appropriate striving embodied in some subservient task, whereas sitting, standing, and sleeping do not. But one of the main points of Ryle's distinction is, after all, to class knowing with the achievements, and knowing does *not* normally presuppose an appropriate investigative striving or inquiry procedure. Contrary to the suggestion embodied in Ryle's treatment, it is plausible to hold that most of what we know, we have not set ourselves to find out.

The general contrast between tasks and achievements, as intended by Ryle, seems thus quite obscure. (It is worth noting the nature of the main difficulties: we found many performances being classed as achievements, but we did not find achievements being turned into performances.) Perhaps the best course is to give up construing the contrast as an absolute and general distinction between two classes, whether of words or of things. We might still intelligibly speak of an achievement-task *relationship* as holding between two verbs, or word-uses, or even nonlinguistic things. We could no longer make lists of verbs as being absolutely achievement verbs or task verbs, but we could relate pairs of verbs as standing in the requisite relationship, and allow the same verb to relate quite differently to others. At any rate, such a relativization of the distinction would be sufficient for the epistemological point which Ryle wants to make: Knowing is an achievement relative to trying to find out or striving to know, and is not itself a task relative to anything else (it itself involves no trying). The fact that *knowing* is not susceptible to mistake thus gives no ground for supposing that *striving to know*, or any other mental task, is infallible, that is, necessarily immune to failure.

THE ATTACK ON INFALLIBLE METHOD

Ryle's critique of infallibility is more limited than classical empiricist critiques. Ryle argues, as we have seen, that to fail to recognize the achievement character of knowing is to tend to engender a belief in the infallibility of some sort of investigative performance. Accordingly, to avoid the critical category-mistake of assimilating achievements to performances is to undercut one argument in favor of such infallibility. It is not, however, to undercut *all* such arguments. On this score, classical empiricism went much further: It argued against the very possibility of infallible assurances of truth in the realm of empirical inquiry. The chief source for such an argument is David Hume, and we shall briefly present some of the ideas in his *Enquiry Concerning Human Understanding,* Section IV (Parts I and II) and Section V (Part I).

Hume divides all "objects of human reason or enquiry" into two kinds: relations of ideas and matters of fact. To the first kind belong geometry, algebra, and arithmetic,

> and in short, every affirmation which is either intuitively or demonstratively certain. *That the square of the hypothenuse is equal to the squares of the two sides,* is a proposition which expresses a relation between these figures. *That three times five is equal to the half of thirty,* expresses a relation between these numbers. Propositions of this kind are discoverable by the mere operation of thought, without dependence on what is anywhere

existent in the universe. Though there never were a circle or triangle in nature, the truths demonstrated by Euclid would forever retain their certainty and evidence.

On the other hand, matters of fact are, according to Hume,

not ascertained in the same manner; nor is our evidence of their truth, however great, of a like nature with the foregoing. The contrary of every matter of fact is still possible; because it can never imply a contradiction, and is conceived by the mind with the same facility and distinctness, as if ever so conformable to reality. *That the sun will not rise tomorrow* is no less intelligible a proposition, and implies no more contradiction than the affirmation, *that it will rise.* We should in vain, therefore, attempt to demonstrate its falsehood. Were it demonstratively false, it would imply a contradiction, and could never be distinctly conceived by the mind.

Empirical truths are, then, neither themselves intuitively certain nor demonstrable—that is, derivable by thought alone from truths whose contraries are self-contradictory. What sort of evidence, then, supports our beliefs concerning matters of fact? Clearly some appeal to the senses and to memory is required, but this is hardly sufficient, for we believe all sorts of empirical propositions whose content reaches far beyond what is presently under observation or presently remembered. Hume argues that we need, in addition, to acknowledge "the relation of Cause and Effect," which enables us to extend our knowledge enormously beyond the immediate contents of sense and memory.

All reasonings concerning matters of fact seem to be founded on the relation of *Cause and Effect.* By means of that relation alone we can go beyond the evidence of our memory and senses. If you were to ask a man, why he believes any matter of fact, which is absent; for instance, that his friend is in the country, or in France; he would give you a reason; and this reason would be some other fact; as a letter received from him, or the knowledge of his former resolutions and promises. A man finding a watch or any other machine in a desert island, would conclude that there had once been men in that island. All our reasonings concerning fact are of the same nature. And here it is constantly supposed that there is a connexion between the present fact and that which is inferred from it. Were there nothing to bind them together, the inference would be entirely precarious.

But how, now, do we arrive at knowledge of cause and effect? Here Hume argues that no certainty can possibly underlie our causal knowledge. "I shall venture to affirm, as a general proposition, which admits of no exception, that the knowledge of this relation is not, in any instance, attained by reasonings *a priori;* but arises entirely from experience, when we find that any particular objects are constantly conjoined with each other." What is the basis, however, of the generalization of conjunctions found in our past experience? "The bread, which I formerly eat, nourished me; that is, a body of such sensible qualities was, at that time, endued with such secret powers: but does it follow, that other bread must also nourish me at another time, and that like sensible qualities must always be attended with like secret powers? The consequence seems nowise necessary. . . . These two propositions are far from being the same, *I have found that such an object has always been attended with such an effect,* and *I foresee, that other objects, which are, in appearance, similar, will be attended with similar effects.*"

Can we *demonstrate* that generalizing from experience is trustworthy? No such demonstration is possible, says Hume, "since it implies no contradiction that the course of nature may change, and that an object, seemingly like those which we have experienced, may be attended with different or contrary effects." Then perhaps, short of *demonstration*, we can offer some other argument for the trustworthiness of generalizing upon experience. But any such argument, since it is short of demonstration, will need itself to be an argument of a probable sort, based on matters of fact—for instance, on our past successes in generalizing. If so, any such argument will be circular, for it will itself be generalizing upon past experience, "taking that for granted, which is the very point in question."

Hume concludes that *no* argument can justify causal generalization or induction, which underlies all reasoning in matters of fact. Another principle needs to be called in, and that is "Custom or Habit," conceived as "a principle of human nature." To form a belief in accordance with a generalization from experience "is an operation of the soul, . . . as unavoidable as to feel the passion of love, when we receive benefits; or hatred, when we meet with injuries. All these operations are a species of natural instincts, which no reasoning or process of the thought and understanding is able either to produce or prevent."

Hume thus provides a general argument against the possibility of an infallible method for ascertaining matters of fact. In addition, he poses the problem of justifying induction, a problem which has had a long and complicated career and with which we shall not deal in this place. The important point for us to note is that the very notion of a certain or infallible empirical method is here attacked head-on. This general attack has been widely accepted by modern schools of philosophy, which have, in one or another way, attempted to provide a plausible account of the probabilistic and tentative character of the growing empirical sciences. Hume's own words on this matter are still relevant:

> The utmost effort of human reason is to reduce the principles, productive of natural phenomena, to a greater simplicity, and to resolve the many particular effects into a few general causes, by means of reasonings from analogy, experience, and observation. But as to the causes of these general causes, we should in vain attempt their discovery; nor shall we ever be able to satisfy ourselves, by any particular explication of them. These ultimate springs and principles are totally shut up from human curiosity and enquiry. . . . The most perfect philosophy of the natural kind only staves off our ignorance a little longer. . . .

Those who have followed Hume thus far have, however, divided on a further issue, with respect to the problem of certainty. Rejecting infallible *knowledge of causal connections*, some have affirmed, while others have denied, that a special sort of certainty attaches to mere *empirical description*. Recall that the main brunt of Hume's argument was directed against the notion that causal *relationships* can be ascertained through a priori reasoning. He addressed particular attention to the *connection* between "the present fact and that which is inferred from it," arguing that nothing so inferred can be guaranteed true in advance. But what about the present fact itself?

Imagine, following Hume's example, that I have just now found a watch on a desert island and proceeded to infer the previous presence of men. Granted Hume's argument with respect to my *inference*, what is the status of the *present fact*, represented by my statement, "This object is a watch"? The negation of this statement is perfectly self-consistent, unlike the case of logical or arithmetical truths, so it is not *logically necessary*. Nonetheless it *is* firmly based on the present testimony of my senses, which I *cannot* now deny. Except for mistaken inferences which I may draw from it, how can I possibly go wrong? For all that Hume says, it appears reasonable to hold such a statement of *present fact* to be *incorrigible* if not necessary: There seems no room whatever for it to be in error, even though it is not *logically* self-evident. In inferring something *else* from a present fact, I must indeed allow that I may turn out to be wrong, but insofar as I simply describe *this* present fact, then no matter what else happens with respect to other presumed facts, no matter how the course of nature may change from its previous patterns, I cannot (it would seem) turn out to be wrong, for my *description* does not commit itself to anything beyond what I now sense or observe. In the descriptive core of my empirical assertions, then, I attain after all a kind of certainty or immunity from error.

Is it true, however, that the statement "This object is a watch" simply limits itself to what I now sense or observe? The statement, after all, purports to refer to a physical object, with a life of its own beyond the boundaries of my present experience. Hume, however, construed purported physical object references themselves as complex references to experienced phenomenal elements—i.e., impressions and ideas. His notion was that all our mental perceptions are either quite lively and forcible, and these he called *impressions*, or else less lively and forcible, and these he called *thoughts or ideas*, which are all copies of *impressions*. All terms in our discourse may be traced to originating impressions if they have an idea or meaning behind them.[4] The notion of a *substance* is simply a "collection of simple ideas . . . united by the imagination."[5] Phenomenalist thinkers, following this line, would accordingly maintain that to say this is a watch is to say only that certain visual, tactual, and other phenomena exist and are associated in a certain way.

Nonetheless, these phenomena are surely *not* all given at the same moment, and this is the important point. To say "This *seems* to be a watch" or "It *seems* as if I am seeing a watch" may indeed be merely to describe currently experienced visual phenomena or "impressions." By contrast, to say "This *is* a watch" is, even for the phenomenalist to say much more; it is to say also, for example, that *if* I have the impression of reaching my hand in a certain direction, I will then have a certain tactual impression; *if* I have the continued impression of looking in the same direction, the visual appearance of the watch will *not* suddenly evaporate; and so on. In other words, the phenomenal analysis of physical object statements agrees with the usual interpretation in taking them as having a reference which extends beyond my momentary experience, since it acknowledges that they are *implicitly predictive*. The upshot is that there is again room for error, even when I simply *describe* current physical facts, for I am, on any account, also committing myself thereby to an indefinitely large number of conditional predictions of further events, which may or may not occur, so far as I can now determine.

Phenomenalists have, however, often argued that judgments of *present phenomenal facts* are quite obviously different in this regard, and that *they are* therefore immune from error. For if I restrict myself to saying, "It *seems to me* as if I were seeing a watch," I have no way of going wrong, provided I am being truthful and trying to describe my experience accurately. For *no matter what else happens*, my statement does not and cannot conflict with it; it is *not* implicitly predictive.

Even if I am dreaming or hallucinating, my description is not put in jeopardy. Hume himself says with regard to impressions that it is not "easy to fall into any error or mistake with regard to them";[6] many phenomenalists have boldly said that phenomenal statements *are certain.*[7]

It should be noted that such certainty is, in any case, not very powerful, for when I come to consider my present phenomenal judgment in the future and try to decide *then* whether it had been true or false, I shall, at that time, need to rely on memory and inference backward from my future phenomenal experiences. Thus, the certainty of my present judgment is a momentary and transient thing at best; it does not, in particular, mean that my judgment will forever carry the same assurance it does now. Nonetheless, is it not the case that, at *each* moment, my sincere attempt at simultaneous phenomenal description is certain to be correct? Am I not still assured that my present judgment of my phenomenal experience *must* be true, even if this assurance cannot extend into the future?[8]

This last argument for infallibility has been criticized by philosophers who point out that we are often undecided as to how to describe our *present* experiences;[9] moreover, we often decide reasonably that a previous description of experience was *mistaken.* The point is not merely that a future assessment of my present judgment will need to rely on inference, and will thus fall short of maximum assurance, but that it may reasonably issue in the conclusion that I am *now mistaken.* I may, for example, be undecided as to whether to say I now have a twinge or a pain in my tooth; having called it a pain, I may later decide it was really a twinge. At that later time, I may have to choose between my present judgment that the feeling in question is a pain and my future judgment that it is exactly similar to the future phenomenal feeling of a twinge in the same place. But if my phenomenal judgments themselves can thus *conflict,* how can I, *even now,* be *sure* that it is my present ones which are true?

Suppose, moreover, that I infer from a purportedly given phenomenal experience that another experience of a certain sort will occur: here Hume insists that the *inference* is shaky because the generalization on which it rests goes beyond my past experience of a finite number of relevant conjunctions. His point is that *even if* the initial phenomenal experience is correctly described, the inferred experience is not bound to occur, for the generalization may be false. It does not, however, follow that the initial experience must of necessity *have been* correctly described. In fact, if the inferred experience fails to occur, I may reasonably decide to uphold the generalization and to judge that my original phenomenal description was in error. In the face of such a real possibility, how can I *even now* be certain that my *present* phenomenal descriptions *are* true? To be sure, *if* they are true, then no other phenomena than certain *present* ones are required for them to be true, but it does not follow that I can therefore be sure that they *are* true. No matter how firm they now seem, they may be dislodged by sufficiently strong competing descriptions which also have a claim on my acceptance. Such dislodging must, of course, itself take place *in the future*, in the form of a future judgment of present error, but this is sufficient to undermine my present absolute assurance. Were it not so, the thesis of phenomenal certainty would rest on the triviality that my present phenomenal judgments cannot *simultaneously* be dislodged. Since, however, *no* actual judgment at a given time can simultaneously be dislodged, such a criterion would render *all* judgments certain and thus empty the notion of certainty of all content. Arguments such as these bring out the *systematic* context of judgments and stress the fact that no statement, physical or phenomenal, can be construed as an isolated unit, absolutely immune from error.[10]

The phenomenalist arguments we have considered defend, at best, only a weak and transient kind of certainty, while the counter-arguments we have cited tend to discredit even this weak variety and thus to suggest that all empirical statements whatever are fallible. We have, in sum, very strong grounds for rejecting the notion that knowing always entails certainty, either in the sense of an infallible method of inquiry or in the sense of an incorrigible form of judgment.

FALLIBILISM AND ABSOLUTE TRUTH

Many philosophers in recent times have argued that once *certainty* is given up as a condition of knowing, *truth* must also be given up, at least in the absolute sense in which every statement is unequivocally true or false, irrespective of time, place, person, and circumstance. The motivations for this argument are various and complex, but a main common purpose has been to bring epistemology into line with scientific practice, in which ideas are treated as fallible hypotheses, subject always to future test. The moral has been drawn that there is, in science, no absolute truth just because there is, in science, no pretension to certainty at any given time. Theories are radically altered in the course of scientific inquiry, and their truth must therefore always be construed as relative to the data and assumptions of the scientific community at a given time.

This general idea has been adopted and debated by several philosophers; it has also frequently been voiced by scientists and has filtered into the opinions of the public. We shall, however, concentrate, in our ensuing discussion, on the formulations of the pragmatic school, since pragmatism has been extremely influential not only in philosophy but also in the realm of education.

Pragmatism should, however, not be construed as a unitary system but rather as a group of related themes and doctrines, interpreted somewhat differently by different pragmatists. We must, in particular, distinguish between pragmatic approaches to *meaning*, which are relatively uniform, and pragmatic approaches to *truth*, which vary importantly in different formulations. We turn first to the pragmatic doctrine of meaning, due to C. S. Peirce,[11] whose purpose was to clarify philosophical thought by bringing to bear the laboratory habit of mind.

Peirce proposed to effect such clarification, specifically, by tying ideas both to their associated *operations* and to their observable *consequences*. He thus opposed the rationalistic approach, which advocated introspection as a way of achieving "clear and distinct ideas," and which sought certainty through subjecting all beliefs to the ordeal of an initial radical doubt. Peirce argued that such universal radical doubt is impossible, its conception a philosopher's fantasy. In real life, our doubts arise piecemeal: we never doubt more than one or a few items at a time, meanwhile taking a mass of beliefs provisionally for granted. In science, the researcher doubts and tests a particular hypothesis, assuming a whole variety of beliefs during the process of test. Afterwards, when new problems arise, he may, of course, return to doubt any of his earlier assumptions. But one thing he cannot do, and that is to doubt all beliefs simultaneously, making no assumptions whatever. Assumptions, in this view, are not rock-bottom foundations; they need not be absolutely guaranteed in advance: Peirce insists on *fallibilism* throughout. The function of assumptions is to give us provisional guidance in action, to help us resolve particular doubts while they themselves are held constant. They are tools to be applied, and their usefulness shows up in the process of their application.

Analogously, in clarifying *particular ideas*, we cannot rely solely on a process of introspection, without considering the application of those ideas in action. For an idea, in the last analysis, relates our action in certain circumstances to specific sensible effects. "Our idea of anything," says Peirce, "*is* our idea of its sensible effects" (p. 124).

Now this is a rather shorthand formulation, for the sensible effects Peirce has in mind are those that result from operations involving the thing in question. Our idea of a *hard* thing, for example, consists of our idea that *if* it is struck, it will make a noise; *if* it is pushed, it will offer a perceptible resistance; and so forth. The general idea of hardness is not to be clarified by introspection, that is, by trying to form an appropriate image, for there is, in this case as in many others, no appropriate image to be found. The idea of hardness relates certain hypothetical actions or operations to certain sensible consequences in an "if-then" manner, and the process of clarification is the process of spelling out these if-then relationships. The trait of hardness possessed by the stone is analogous to a habit, that is to say, it is a disposition to respond sensibly in certain ways, under specific circumstances. Like a habit, it is not capable of representation by an image, since it consists in an abstract and general connection of circumstances and responses. It may indeed be questioned whether this account is capable of complete generalization, for the idea of some sensible effect itself—for example, *redness*—may seem to denote a specific imaginable quality, rather than an abstract connection. We shall not try to settle this issue, for, in any event, there is an enormous class of ideas, and these the most in need of clarification, which cannot, by any stretch of the imagination, be construed as denoting sensible qualities in experience. We shall take Peirce as addressing himself to these in formulating his maxim of pragmatic method.

"Consider," says Peirce, in stating this maxim, "what effects, which might conceivably have practical bearings, we conceive the object of our conception to have. Then, our conception of these effects is the whole of our conception of the object" (p. 124). Our conception or idea of hardness—for example, represented by the adjective *hard*—is just our conception of all those sensible effects resulting from practical operations upon hard things. *Hardness* is exemplified by a variety of sensible effects connected in determinate ways with certain sorts of action, and the *idea of hardness* is nothing more than the idea of these practically contingent effects. It is, thus, specifiable in a set of if-then propositions, each one setting forth some sensible occurrence as a result of a particular operation. Such an if-then proposition has come to be known as an operational definition:[12] in the case of the hardness of minerals, for example, such a definition might be set forth, in simplified form, as follows, with reference to a standard substance *S:*

X is hard = If X is rubbed against the standard substance S, then X scratches S.

An operational definition of *being above average in intelligence* might analogously be framed by reference to an intelligence test *T* as follows:

X is above average in intelligence = If X takes the test T, then X scores above 110.

When we turn from the clarification of *particular ideas*, represented by terms such as "hard," to the clarification of *whole statements*, e.g., "This stone is hard," we approach the level of belief. For belief is embodied not in particular ideas or terms but rather in whole statements, or the propositions they may be taken to express. What, then, does it mean to believe that this stone is hard? If a person has this belief, says Peirce, *he* has a certain habit of action with respect to the stone; he is set to act toward it in accordance with *its* supposed habit of hardness. He is prepared to act toward it in certain ways, should he wish to produce certain sensible effects. For example, should he wish to make a mark on some surface composed of the standard substance, *S*, he is set to use the stone as a marking instrument. "The whole function of thought," says Peirce, "is to produce habits of action. . . . Now, the identity of a habit depends on how it might lead us to act, not merely under such circumstances as are likely to arise, but under such as might possibly occur, no matter how improbable they may be. . . . There is no distinction of meaning so fine as to consist in anything but a possible difference of practice" (p. 123).

A statement has meaning, one might say, just insofar as it is capable of expressing a belief, capable therefore of representing a habit of action involving perceptual stimuli and sensible results. To have meaning, in short, it must embody conditional predictions testable by the senses. Peirce allows, of course, that false as well as true beliefs have meaning, but the processes of scientific investigation continually weed the false beliefs out and bring scientists to convergence on the true. Indeed, he defines truth in terms of such ultimate and ideal convergence. "Different minds," he writes, "may set out with the most antagonistic views, but the progress of investigation carries them by a force outside of themselves to one and the same conclusion. This activity of thought by which we are carried, not where we wish, but to a foreordained goal, is like the operation of destiny. No modification of the point of view taken, no selection of other facts for study, no natural bent of mind even, can enable a man to escape the predestinate opinion. This great law is embodied in the conception of truth and reality. The opinion which is fated to be ultimately agreed to by all who investigate is what we mean by the truth, and the object represented in this opinion is the real. That is the way I would explain reality" (p. 133).

The notion of truth here presented is an ideal and purportedly absolute one: As Peirce remarks, "the opinion which would finally result from investigation does not depend on how anybody may actually think" (p. 134). To the possible objection that there are enormously many facts of history long lost and forever beyond the reach of further investigation, Peirce replies that it is not possible to be sure that any given fact might not be revealed by continuing science, for science has already brought to light numerous facts previously thought impossible to know. Does not such a reply rest, however, on "remote considerations," especially in view of the "principle that only practical distinctions have a meaning"? (p. 135) Peirce indeed confesses their remoteness, but suggests that his doctrine enables a clear apprehension of the object and procedures of science. He seems to be saying that only if we think of truth as a fixed ideal of scientific method can we make sense of the fact that scientific controversies are often settled in the course of time, apparently under the control of impersonal and objective factors. It must be admitted that Peirce's account of truth does not lend itself readily to formulation in terms of his own theory of "operational definition." It seems, rather, motivated by his desire to make sense of scientific method, by projecting an ideal limit toward which it is directed.

It may be argued that Peirce's theory of truth is thus inconsistent with his stated method for clarifying particular ideas. However that may be, there seem to be independent weaknesses in his account of truth.[13] We may note, to begin with, that his reference to truth as a "foreordained goal" (p. 133) which no man can escape cannot be taken literally. Certainly, there have always been radical disagreements in science as elsewhere; how could it possibly be known that fate decrees an ultimate settlement? Peirce himself allows that, "Our perversity and that of others may indefinitely postpone the settlement of opinion; it might even conceivably cause an arbitrary proposition to be universally accepted as long as the human race should last. Yet," he continues, "even that would not change the nature of the belief, which alone could be the result of investigation carried sufficiently far; and if, after the extinction of our race, another should arise with faculties and disposition for investigation, that true opinion must be the one which they would ultimately come to. 'Truth crushed to earth shall rise again.' . . ." (pp. 133–134).

What gives Peirce the assurance that settlement must ultimately fix upon the truth? It is surely not logically contradictory to suppose that it never does, even on the assumption of endless investigation. His reference to "investigation carried sufficiently far" of course gives him the option of denying that, so long as disagreement remains, investigation has been sufficient. But, then, the assertion: that agreement must come after sufficient investigation, is *empty,* since it reduces to the claim that agreement must be the result of investigation that is sufficient to achieve agreement.

Peirce is impressed with the control of scientific assertions by objective criteria, and it is this, we have suggested, which drives him to interpret truth as independent of what any particular man may think. On the other hand, he wants, generally, to reduce everything to what is accessible to thought. He thus construes truth as the agreed object of "thought in general" (p. 133), i.e., endless investigation by the community of science. Yet what rules out the possibility that perfect agreement *is* reached on a falsehood, and is never reversed? If, for instance, an erroneous account of some particular historical event long past has been propagated and gotten entrenched, never to be revised until the end of time, must it be *true* and must it therefore represent *reality*? Peirce's argument is that we cannot be sure that such an opinion will *not* be revised, but, equally, he cannot be sure that it *will*, and indeed it seems to fly in the face of all probabilities to *assume* that it will, in every case. To say that it *would*, if investigation were "carried far enough" (p. 134) is, in the absence of an independent criterion for the notion of "far enough," to reduce the claim to triviality. To admit, on the other hand, that it is *conceivable* that there might be facts *not* revealed by investigation, or that there might be purported facts *erroneously* revealed, is to acknowledge that investigation itself is not the final determinant of truth—that the agreement of investigators is valuable only if it satisfies the independent condition of accurate representation of the facts.

THE ABSOLUTENESS OF TRUTH

On the question of truth, there is considerable variation among pragmatists. Whereas Peirce offers an ideal and absolute notion of truth, as we have seen, William James formulates a practical and relative interpretation. Paradoxically, however, while Peirce's doctrine seems to be at odds with his own pragmatic method for the clarifying of particular ideas, James' theory represents an attempt to clarify the particular idea *true* by means of this very method. James needs, accordingly, to specify a relevant *operation* with respect to belief and to indicate a class of *sensible effects* associated with this operation whenever it is applied to beliefs which are *true*.[14]

In this context, he suggests the "operation" of acting on a belief, his general idea being that if, and only if, a belief is *true*, will it yield sensibly satisfactory results in experience when thus acted upon. What sorts of things, however, fall under the rubric of satisfactory results? James' account is rather vague. In a typical passage, he writes,

> Any idea upon which we can ride, so to speak; any idea that will carry us prosperously from any one part of our experience to any other part, linking things satisfactorily, working securely, simplifying, saving labor; is true for just so much, true in so far forth, true *instrumentally*.[15]

Unfortunately, such passages seem to allow room for a *broad* as well as a *narrow* construction, as regards the sort of satisfaction to be correlated with truth. On the narrow construction, a belief functions satisfactorily when it is satisfied or confirmed by experience. On the broad interpretation, satisfactory function includes also such satisfying effects of belief on the believer as, for example, pleasant or comfortable states of mind, constructive attitudes toward life, and healthy traits of character.

Moreover, it is difficult to interpret several of James' own passages without appealing to the broad notion of satisfaction. For example, James writes, "If theological ideas prove to have a value for concrete life, they will be true, for pragmatism, in the sense of being good for so much"; in previous and later paragraphs, he indicates that by "value for concrete life" he includes the "religious comfort" yielded "to a most respectable class of minds" (pp. 71–73). Referring to belief in the Absolute, he writes, "so far as it affords such comfort, it surely is not sterile; it has that amount of value; it performs a concrete function. As a good pragmatist, I myself ought to call the Absolute true 'in so far forth', then; and I unhesitatingly now do so" (p. 73).

James then goes on to criticize belief in the Absolute because it conflicts in other areas with other truths having "vital benefit." But the crucial point is that he takes the religious comfort afforded by a belief as one sort of "vital benefit," as one count in favor of its truth. Generalizing, he says,

> If there be any life that it is really better we should lead, and if there be any idea which, if believed in, would help us to lead that life, then it would be really *better for us* to believe in that idea, *unless, indeed, belief in it incidentally clashed with other greater vital benefits.* "What would be better for us to believe"! This sounds very like a definition of truth (pp. 76–77).

James surely is *not* guilty of allowing the pleasantness of a belief to override all other considerations, and he rightly rejects criticisms to the effect that the pragmatist calls "everything true which, if it were true, would be pleasant" (p. 234). But it seems undeniable that he does take pleasantness or comfort as *one* evidence of truth. It is this that remains subject to criticism, since the effects of a belief on the believer are altogether irrelevant to the question whether or not the belief is true. What counts at all is whether things are indeed as the belief asserts them to be, and clearly this is logically independent of the psychological effects of accepting the belief. If truth is, as James says, "one species of good" (p. 75), this particular good (or satisfaction) needs to be narrowly circumscribed. The narrow interpretation of James' theory is addressed, indeed, not to psychological consequences of belief acceptance that are satisfactory in the sense of being pleasant but rather to logical consequences of the accepted belief that are satisfactory in the sense of being borne out by experience.

The latter idea forms the basis of a less objectionable version of James' theory of truth; the satisfactory character of a true belief consists in its predictive adequacy: Given that a belief is true, then, and only then, if you act on this belief, forming your predictions in accordance with it, experience will satisfy *these predictions*, it being irrelevant whether or not *you* are satisfied also. The satisfaction of a prediction by experience represents a verification of the belief upon which this prediction rests. Truth is, then, a function of particular verifications, and its value lies in its preparing us adequately to face our future experience.

> Truth for us [says James] is simply a collective name for verification-processes, just as health, wealth, strength, etc., are names for other processes connected with life, and also pursued because it pays to pursue them. Truth is *made*, just as health, wealth and strength are made, in the course of experience (p. 218).

The formulation of James' theory in terms of verification-processes escapes the criticism that psychological satisfaction is taken as an index of truth. In the last sentence of the passage just quoted, however, we find evidence of a fundamental *relativism* in the present version of James' theory, which occasions further difficulties. James in fact insists that truth is not a "timeless quality" (p. 219) but rather something that appears in the historic process as a concomitant of verification. Thus, James writes, "ideas (which themselves are but parts of our experience) become true just in so far as they help us to get into satisfactory relation with other parts of our experience . . ." (p. 58). In another place, he expresses his point still more directly, as follows, "The truth of an idea is not a stagnant property inherent in it. Truth *happens* to an idea. It *becomes* true, is *made* true by events. Its verity *is* in fact an event, a process: the process namely of its verifying itself, its veri-*fication*" (p. 201).

The general notion is one that has been proposed by many thinkers in recent times: we are to construe truth not as an absolute property of ideas but rather as a variable property—that is, as one which is relative to time and person, for it is to be correlated with verification or confirmation, which is itself relative to time and person. A major motivation for this view, as we remarked earlier, is to bring truth into line with the spirit and practice of science, the supposition being that an absolute notion of truth leads to dogmatism. As James puts it,

> the great assumption of the intellectualists is that truth means essentially an inert static relation. When you've got your true

idea of anything, there's an end of the matter. You're in possession; you *know;* you have fulfilled your thinking destiny (p. 200).

There seems, however, to be a fundamental confusion here between *absolute truth* and *certainty.* It is one thing to believe that truth is an absolute, i.e., unvarying property of ideas or beliefs; it is quite another to suppose that we can ever be certain that we have the truth. Accordingly, it is logically quite possible to deny certainty and yet to uphold an absolute theory of truth. The spirit and practice of science are indeed opposed to dogmatism, but dogmatism rests on a conviction of certainty, not absolute truth. We have already seen, in fact, how Peirce combined a doctrine of fallibilism, inspired by science, with a notion of truth as an ideal and unvarying limit of scientific investigation. Clearly, we have, at any given time, ideas or beliefs we *estimate as true* or *take to be true. These* are surely altered in the course of our experience; it does not follow at all that the *truth itself* is altered or alterable. James may perhaps be interpreted as essentially interested in attacking certainty; he is then on firm ground, though still mistaken in formulating his doctrine as an attack on absolute truth.[16]

There are, moreover, several *independent* arguments against relativizing truth through reduction to the concepts of verification or confirmation. We typically suppose a statement to be either true or false (in accord with the *principle of excluded middle*). But some statements are neither confirmed nor disconfirmed for given persons at given times. We cannot now, for instance, confirm nor disconfirm Caesar's having had breakfast the day he crossed the Rubicon. Yet we must acknowledge that he either did or did not, and, accordingly, that it is either true that he did or true that he did not, even though we do not know which it is.

We also suppose (in accord with the *law of contradiction*) that no statement can be both true and false. Yet some statements clearly are confirmed for some persons in some circumstances and not for others in the same or other circumstances. Imagine, for example, that I have a toothache but am sufficiently skilled in hiding my feelings from my family to avoid giving them any inkling of my suffering. They will then have good reason to deny that I have a toothache, while I will have excellent, and painful, grounds for affirming that I do. Yet it cannot be both true and false that I have a toothache.

Consider, now, the case of a *change* in the degree of confirmation of an idea, over time. If, in particular, a scientific theory has proved itself predictively adequate throughout a given period and has then been decisively disconfirmed, we do not describe it as having first been true and as having then become false. We may, however, say it had, for a time, been *taken as* true, and then been *judged to be* false. Otherwise, we should be driven to suppose that nature itself changes along with our changing theories, and that the latter do not really conflict: So long as Newtonian theory was predictively satisfactory, it was true—that is, nature *was* Newtonian; with the breakdown of Newtonianism, nature ceased its Newtonian ways and has since become Einsteinian. To be sure, nature may change, but what reason is there to believe that it changes obediently every time a new physical theory achieves dominance?

Furthermore, since each such theory purports to describe not merely large regions of nature but what is *always* and *everywhere* the case, it is logically absurd to hold that first one and then a quite different one is true. Historical examples are even more striking: It used to be thought that Galileo dropped iron balls from the leaning tower of Pisa. It is nowadays held that this story is a myth. Now we cannot suppose that it was for a time true that Galileo did drop iron balls from the tower and then it became true that he never did. Either he did at some time or he never did; the truth in this matter is not mutable, though, of course, our *opinions* as to what the truth is *are* surely subject to change.[17]

James himself seems less than consistent on these points. He wants to say, on the one hand, that earlier theories *were* true within their "borders of experience" (p. 223) and that earlier processes were "truth-processes for the actors in them" (p. 224) though not for us. Yet, on the other hand, he also says that our retrospective judgments *were true* despite earlier thinkers, shedding a "backward light" (pp. 223–224) on the past; he even admits that the views of earlier thinkers are false "absolutely"—he puts quotation marks around the word—(p. 223) since the borders of their experience *might* conceivably have been transcended. Indeed, all he succeeds in showing is that what is *taken to be true* changes from time to time with the progress of investigation, but he seems to acknowledge that whatever *is taken to be true* is taken to be true *absolutely*, for there are (as we have seen) difficulties in *taking* the same idea to be now true, now false. In sum, variability characterizes *estimation of* the truth, not truth itself.

It is important to distinguish the absoluteness of truth from the fixity of natural processes, for the two ideas are quite independent. Truth is an attribute of statements, beliefs, propositions, or ideas, not an attribute of things, processes, or events generally. To say that truth is absolute is to say that *whatever* true statements or ideas affirm is unqualifiedly in fact the case; no further requirement is made that true statements must affirm only *constancies* or *fixities*. The facts of change, whatever they may be, render their true descriptions true absolutely. Fluid historical processes or transient historical events do not require fluidity or transiency in the truth of their true descriptions: We have already seen the absurdity of supposing it to be initially true and thereafter false that Galileo at some point in time dropped iron balls from the tower of Pisa. Conversely, the absolute truth of the statement that the First World War began in 1914 does not imply that the First World War's beginning is somehow timeless and fixed, that the War is, somehow, always in a state of incipiency. Spatial as well as temporal qualifications of all sorts apply to things describable by true statements, but this does not imply that the truth itself must be similarly qualified. If it rained in Mexico City on April 7, 1934, the sentence "It rained in Mexico City on April 7, 1934" is not just true in Mexico City; it is simply true. Analogously, it is not just true on April 7, 1934; it is simply true. Insofar, then, as a relativistic doctrine of truth is motivated by the desire to stress the "fluidity" of history and the pervasiveness of natural change, the same purpose can perfectly well (and with enormously less logical strain) be accomplished by an absolute doctrine of truth.

It may, however, in spite of all we have said, be objected that there is a particular class of statements whose *truth* clearly does change with time, place, or person. Consider the following three sentences, for example:

    (i) Today is Sunday.
    (ii) This city has three daily newspapers.
    (iii) I am a Republican.

Clearly neither (i), nor (ii), nor (iii) is invariably true. (i) is true only on Sundays. (ii) is true only in such cities as have three daily newspapers. (iii) is true only when said by a Republican.

It may, in reply, be said that these sentences are all, in a basic sense, incomplete or indeterminate. They do not, in themselves, succeed in making definite assertions, for the grammatical subjects of their respective attributions, i.e., *Today, This city,* and *I,* have no fixed references. How can any of these sentences be evaluated for truth, when it is not clear to what thing its attribution is being made? Suppose one said "*X* is a Republican." Would it be anything more than the *schema* of an assertion? Surely such a schema has no fixed truth or falsity (no fixed truth-value, to put it briefly) but may be transformed into an indefinite number of statements with fixed truth-values when the variable "*X*" is replaced by a name or description, or when the whole is prefixed by "For all *X*," or "There is an *X,* such that." The absolute theory of truth is not a denial that *schemas* are thus variable with respect to truth, but schemas should not be confused with genuine assertions or statements.

It is of course true that (i), (ii), and (iii) are, in one sense, more determinate than schemas with variables such as *"X," "Y,"* etc. The word *today,* for example, though it varies in reference, as does *"X,"* nonetheless *acquires* a definite reference *in the context of its utterance,* unlike *"X."* That is to say, when a particular speaker assertively utters the words "Today is Sunday," *today* refers to the day on which this particular utterance itself falls. Analogously, *this city* refers, on the occasion of utterance, to the city in which the utterance takes place, and *I* refers, when uttered, to the speaker who utters it. Nevertheless, the forms (i), (ii), and (iii), considered apart from utterance, do not succeed in making an assertion any more than does a pure schema. Moreover, as soon as such a form does yield an assertion, through actual *utterance,* not only do its purported references become determinate, but its truth-value is fixed. The utterance, *on a given occasion,* of "Today is Sunday" is thus true or false absolutely, even though the same form of words makes a different assertion when uttered on another day.

The variable indicator words,[18] *today, this, I,* and so forth, may of course be supplanted altogether by nonindicator expressions with definite references; in this way, a fixed truth-value is attained which is preserved even when the same form of words is repeated in other circumstances. When "Eisenhower is a Republican" thus replaces Mr. Eisenhower's own utterance "I am a Republican," its truth-value is fixed not only as an utterance but as a repeatable form of words. The general point is clear: Provided we have a genuine statement or assertion, its truth-value is fixed.

A peculiarity of the notion of absolute truth is that it seems to be totally "transparent," i.e., to add nothing to the facts in question. *That's true* is, like *yes,* just a mode of assent to a statement understood in context; it is a way of re-asserting the statement itself without literally repeating it. Further, the sentence "It is true that Columbus discovered America" seems to say nothing more than *Columbus discovered America;* the prefix *It is true that* is just a device to provide emphasis. Finally, even where we make *attributions* or *predications* of truth, as, for example, in "The statement 'Columbus discovered America' is true," or "The first statement on page 374 of Volume 7 of the Britannica is true," we seem to be affirming nothing more than what the respectively *mentioned* statements themselves affirm: In each case, both mentioned statement and truth attribution are true together or false together (though in the Britannica example we may not even know in what form of words the mentioned statement consists). The truth attribution is thus itself correct if and only if the sentence to which truth is attributed expresses what is, in fact, the case. The same facts which make the latter sentence true also make the truth attribution itself true.

The "transparency" of absolute truth, though perhaps hard to grasp, involves no fundamental logical difficulties. The logician Alfred Tarski has, in fact, formulated a criterion of truth that incorporates this feature and points up the differentiation of truth from relative notions of confirmation.[19] The criterion of Tarski forms the basis of an explicit argument by R. Carnap that even if we give up the ideal of conclusive confirmation, that is, *certainty*, we need not give up the absolute notion of *truth*.[20] A review of Tarski's proposal and of Carnap's argument will close the present chapter.

Tarski calls his criterion the *semantic criterion of truth*, since it treats truth in the sense of an *attribution* to certain sentences and links it to what is described by those sentences, semantics having to do with the relations between language and reality. His inspiration is Aristotle's doctrine: "To say of what is that it is not, or of what is not that it is, is false, while to say of what is that it is, or of what is not that it is not, is true."[21] Tarski takes this idea to have a modern formulation in the statement: "The truth of a sentence consists in its agreement with (or correspondence to) reality."[22]

In connection with the particular sentence "Snow is white," Tarski says the following equivalence, expressing the requisite correspondence, must hold under any adequate definition of truth:

> The sentence "Snow is white" is true if, and only if, snow is white.

Generalizing, he maintains that all equivalences of the following form must hold:

> "_____" is true if, and
> only if, _____

(provided both blanks are filled by the same sentence, under a fixed interpretation, and belonging to the language of the formula itself). The left blank, having quotation marks around it, forms a *name* of whatever sentence is inserted in it, while the right blank does not. The sentence inserted on the right thus expresses a factual condition or state of affairs which holds if and only if the sentence itself (named on the left) is true. (For the use of quotation marks on the left, any other naming device may, moreover, be substituted, provided it names the sentence on the right.) The formula as a whole represents Tarski's criterion.

This criterion is *not* a definition of truth, for it contains blanks and is thus only a schema, not a statement, while every actual statement formed by filling in its blanks is insufficiently general to serve as a definition. Nonetheless, it represents a condition that must, according to Tarski, be satisfied by any adequate definition of truth.

Any such definition, in other words, needs to be such that all sentences formed in accord with the criterion formula follow from the definition. For our purposes, it is not necessary to go into the technicalities of Tarski's own *definition*, as distinct from his criterion. For the criterion, if it is indeed taken as a necessary condition of truth, is itself sufficient to show the independence of truth from confirmation and to indicate the force of the absolute construal of truth, which it represents.

The criterion, in effect, shows the attribution of truth to a sentence to be tantamount to asserting the sentence itself and hence to be "transparent" in the sense earlier discussed. The criterion offers, however, no method for deciding whether to affirm the sentence in the first instance; it does not tell us, for example, whether snow *is* white. It says only that "whenever we assert or reject this sentence, we must be ready to assert or reject the correlated sentence . . . ' "Snow is white" is true.' "[23] Since true sentences are, however, indefinitely varied, is it any wonder that a unitary method for *ascertaining* truth is a difficult, perhaps impossible, objective? In any event, the criterion is itself sufficient to show that there is no more mystery in truth than in the various sentences themselves asserted to be true. As W. V. Quine has remarked, "Attribution of truth in particular to 'Snow is white', for example, is every bit as clear to us as attribution of whiteness to snow."[24] To put it metaphorically, *truth* is an indirect reflection of the facts themselves, and the *absoluteness of truth* is merely a reflection of the intelligibility of factual descriptions which are not relative to the state of a person's knowledge or belief: We understand perfectly well the question "Is snow white?" and do not need to ask "White for whom?"

Rudolf Carnap, building on Tarski's theory, stresses the difference between truth and confirmation, and the immunity of truth to objections against certainty. Carnap's argument may be presented (in slightly altered form) by reference to the following three sentences:

(i) The substance in the vessel at time *t* is alcohol.
(ii) "The substance in the vessel at time *t* is alcohol" is true.
(iii) *X* believes (confirms, accepts) now, that the sentence
  "The substance in the vessel at time *t* is alcohol" is true.

Following Tarski, (i) holds if, and only if, (ii) does. But the same can clearly not be said of (i) and (iii). For it is obviously possible that the vessel may contain alcohol at *t* while *X* believes (confirms or accepts) now, that the sentence "The substance in the vessel at time *t* is alcohol" is false. Conversely, it is also possible for *X* to hold the sentence in question to be true even though the vessel does not contain alcohol at *t* but rather water. It follows that (ii) also diverges from (iii), for (ii) holds just in those conditions under which (i) does. Thus, the sentence "The substance in the vessel at time *t* is alcohol" may be true but not believed by *X* to be true, and vice versa. Truth is therefore one thing, and being believed, accepted, or confirmed as true is quite another.

Many have argued, says Carnap, that the semantic (or absolute) notion of truth should be abandoned, for scientific purposes at least, since it can never be decided *with certainty* for any empirical sentence *S,* that *S* is true or false. Granted, says Carnap, that such certainty is out of the question, does it follow that truth is therefore inadmissible? Such an inference would apparently hinge on the principle: "A term (predicate) must be rejected if it is such that we can never decide with absolute certainty for any given instance whether or not the term applies."[25] But clearly, argues Carnap, this principle "would lead to absurd consequences." For if we cannot decide the application of *true* in (ii) with certainty, then, by the same token, we cannot decide *alcohol* in (i) with certainty; conversely, if we could be certain about the term *alcohol* in (i), we could equally be certain about *true* in (ii). If we follow the above principle in rejecting *true*, we shall also need to reject all empirical terms as well.

The principle may then be replaced by the following weaker version: "A term (predicate) is a legitimate scientific term . . . if and only if a sentence applying the term to a given instance can possibly be confirmed to at least some degree."[26] The latter version no longer has the absurd consequences of its predecessor. Clearly, it legitimizes the term *alcohol*, but also, by the same token, the term *true*.

The large consequence of the foregoing considerations is that even if we totally reject certainty as a condition of knowledge, we need not also reject (absolute) truth. To attribute knowledge that *Q,* is not only to attribute belief that *Q* but also to affirm that *Q*—in effect, to affirm also that *"Q"* is *true,* in the absolute sense of the term. To be sure, we cannot claim *infallibility* for our knowledge attributions; any of these may turn out to be mistaken. But the latter are no worse in this regard than any of our *other* factual attributions. And if we allow ourselves to make other such attributions, though they are admittedly fallible, how can we deny ourselves the right to make knowledge attributions, in particular?

Since we cannot, in general, be obliged to do what is impossible for us to do, we cannot be obliged to attain certainty in *any* case of empirical fact. We *can,* however, be expected to fashion our attributions in accordance with the evidence available to us, and to treat them as subject to public criticism and to revision upon the emergence of contrary evidence.

The possibility of such revision, *presently* contemplated, is indeed what makes our current factual attributions incapable of absolute assurance. But this bare *possibility* is no reason at all either for controverting the evidence available *now* or for refraining from judgment altogether. When and if contrary evidence emerges, we shall then have good reason to revise our present judgments, but, meanwhile, the mere fact that contrary evidence may emerge later constitutes no reason for present revision. Knowledge attributions, in sum, are no different from other factual attributions with respect to certainty. Our job is not to judge the truth infallibly but to estimate the truth responsibly.

We turn now from discussions of the truth condition of propositional knowledge to a consideration of the evidence condition.

•

CHAPTER THREE

Knowledge and Evidence

•

MOTIVATION FOR THE EVIDENCE CONDITION

In the sample definition of propositional knowledge stated at the end of Chapter I, X was required to have *adequate evidence* that Q, as one condition of his *knowing* that Q. This "evidence condition" was intended to formulate more precisely the idea that knowing in the *strong sense* is more than just true belief, involving also the ability to justify or back up the belief in appropriate manner.

The force of the evidence condition may be illustrated historically by reference to St. Augustine's theory of teaching. Augustine argues against the idea that the teacher transmits *knowledge* through words. Words are signs referring to reality, he says, and knowledge is not a matter simply of having the words. It requires also a personal confrontation with the reality to which the words refer. Without such confrontation, the student may, at best, acquire belief, but not knowledge. The teacher thus cannot be thought literally to be conveying *knowledge* to the student by means of his words. Rather, he *prompts* the student to confront reality for himself, in such a way as to acquire knowledge. "The import of words," says Augustine, "—to state the most that can be said for them—consists in this: they serve merely to suggest that we look for realities" (p. 154).[1] If someone tells me that Q, but I fail to find the realities to which "Q" refers, I can at best believe—I cannot know—that Q. "I do not know all I believe," says Augustine, "But I am not for that reason unaware how useful it is to believe also many things which I do not know" (p. 155). Knowing, for Augustine, is a stronger notion than belief. It comes "not through words sounding in the ear, but through truth that teaches internally" (p. 154). When teachers have explained, he says, "by means of words, all those subjects which they profess to teach, and even the science of virtue and wisdom, then those who are called pupils consider within themselves whether what has been said is true" (p. 158).

The pupil who *knows,* Augustine seems to say, is not just someone who *has a belief which is true,* even if he has the belief on the highest authority (he uses Biblical examples). He must further have considered within himself whether what has been said is true. He must have engaged in a personal process of *evaluating* the belief in question, by reference to his own source of "interior truth." If we consider just this emphasis in Augustine's doctrine, apart from the further metaphysical and religious interpretation which he gives it, we can see the point of the evidence condition. It serves to distinguish genuine knowing from mere true belief, by reference to appropriate evaluation of the belief by the believer: The surplus strength of knowing consists, in short, in the knower's having adequate evidence for the belief in question.

APPRAISING EVIDENTIAL ADEQUACY

If the point of the evidence condition is clear, there are still, however, several features of it that require interpretation. For example, X is required to have adequate evidence that Q, but does this mean simply that there is evidence available to X which is, as a matter of fact, adequate for "Q"? Suppose that "Q" is a generalization which, in X's experience, has broken down decisively in certain instances after having been positively confirmed in an overwhelming number of others. We should not wish to grant that X has, in these circumstances, adequate evidence for "Q," even though he does, as a matter of fact, have an overwhelming number of positive instances, sufficient, in themselves, to provide adequate support for "Q." We should rather maintain that X is obliged to take his clearly *negative* evidence into account as a basis for *rejecting* the generalization in question. If, indeed, he held on to his belief in "Q" in the face of such contrary evidence, then, even supposing such evidence later withdrawn and assuming "Q" to be really true, we should deny that he initially *knew* that "Q" was true.

It appears, then, that we need to put a special interpretation on the condition that X has adequate evidence for "Q": X's *total* evidence must provide adequate support for "Q." *His* total evidence cannot, of course, generally be expected to be the same as *our* total evidence, but the adequacy of his support for "Q" needs to be judged by reference to *every* relevant item of evidence that *he* has; adequacy cannot be bought at the price of ignoring available contrary indications. The totality of evidence available to X may, furthermore, change over time, but the question whether X knows that Q, needs itself, strictly speaking, to be understood as referring to a particular time. Whatever time is in question, it is the totality of X's evidence *at that time* which needs to be adequate.

A second feature of the evidence condition that requires interpretation is its implicit reference to *standards*. Adequacy is, after all, a matter of appraisal, involving standards of judgment that may differ from age to age, from culture to culture, and even from person to person. The variability of such standards does not, however, imply that assessments of knowledge are arbitrary or that the would-be assessor is somehow paralyzed. He needs to assess in accord with his own best standards at the time, but he may hold his assessment subject to change, should he later have cause to revise these standards. The situation is, in principle, no different from other situations involving appraisal.

As in all such situations, too, there is considerable leeway in the *application* of a *given set* of standards in different contexts. For some purposes we may find it expedient to be more stringent; for other purposes we may be more lenient. In appraising a small child's knowledge, we normally apply our standards of evidential adequacy more leniently than in appraising the knowledge of adults. In educative contexts, in particular, our purpose is to develop the child's autonomous appraisals of his own beliefs, by standards of evidence we ourselves hold appropriate. The child's capacity, however, limits the degree to which he can incorporate and apply these standards. To appraise his knowledge, in the context of schooling, serves typically to mark his *advance* within the bounds set by capacity; for this purpose, a relatively lenient application of standards seems *initially* appropriate.

As the child grows, and as his prior learning takes hold, his capacity increases, allowing us to tighten the application of our standards in gauging his current performance. Just as a degree of stringency beyond the child's capacity is inappropriate since it does not allow us to mark his real progress, so a too lenient application of standards, within the minimal ranges of the child's capacity, is inappropriate for the same reason. If knowledge appraisals are to be capable of marking relevant advances, the stringency with which standards are applied needs to keep pace with changing levels of capacity. As capacity grows, the same subject may thus come to be known under ever more stringent interpretations of *known*.

Recapitulation and cyclical development are, thus, important aspects of planning for the teacher and curriculum-maker. We have here indicated their connection with capacity, but there are also other significant factors, of attitude and general maturity, which need to be taken into account in any systematic approach to "the rhythm of education."[2] We have also referred, loosely, to the child's age as an index of capacity, but clearly this is only a rough index, to be tempered by an awareness of individual differences.

` Our concern has been the variability in application of our standards to students' performance. Such variability does not preclude a stringent definition of these standards for the purpose of *setting our own sights* as teachers. From the point of view of such an ideal definition, we can see the whole course of a child's education as involving the progressive incorporation, and increasingly autonomous use, of these standards. From this point of view, too, we may assess the relative level of a child's knowledge by reference to expert adult knowledge.

To sum up, the notion of *adequacy* involves standards, which are normally applied more strictly in some cases, more approximately in others, thus giving rise to multiple interpretations of *knowing;* we need to be aware of such multiplicity so that we can understand or make explicit the relevant interpretation, should the need arise. The implicit appeal to standards of adequacy in knowledge attributions means that, in an important sense, these attributions have a normative function as well as a descriptive one: They attribute *belief* in "*Q*" and affirm the *truth* of "*Q*," but they also *appraise* the believer's grounds for belief, in the light of assumed standards. The knowing attribution thus not only commits the speaker to the beliefs he assigns to another; it also reflects his epistemological commitments—that is, his espousal of certain standards of evidence by which beliefs are to be appraised as well- or ill-grounded.

LIMITS OF EVIDENCE AND THE RIGHT TO BE SURE

We turn now to the more radical question of the correctness of the evidence condition, granted the refinements of the previous section. There seem, in fact, certain important *limits* to the concept of evidence, which may hamper the applicability of the sample definition of knowledge we have been considering.

Take first the cases of mathematical and of moral knowledge. Suppose (i) that X knows that the Pythagorean theorem is true, or (ii) that X knows that some proposed course of action is wrong. The evidence condition requires that X have adequate evidence in each case. If we think of a geometry class, however, what is appropriate to require of X is a *proof*, not evidence; in general, too, mathematicians talk about constructing proofs, not about gathering evidence for or against their assertions. If we think rather of moral deliberation, we take the moral agent to be subject to the demand to furnish *reasons* for his judgment, but we do not suppose every such reason to constitute *evidence;* some such reasons are peculiarly moral reasons. Now this argument has undeniable force as regards the common uses of the term *evidence,* but it can be met by an explicit and admittedly uncommon construal of this term as encompassing proofs and moral reasons as special cases. The notion of *evidence,* for the purpose of the evidence condition, is, then, to be taken as roughly equivalent to that of *good reasons,* or a *good case.* Having adequate evidence for *"Q"* is having a good case, or good reasons, in support of *"Q."* What is demanded in the way of a good case will, of course, vary with the subject: In empirical matters empirical evidence is appropriate; in mathematics it is proofs that count; in moral deliberation, moral reasons have a distinctive role to play.

A second limitation seems to hold for phenomenalistic knowledge, for which even the above broad construal of *evidence* appears inadequate. Consider, as a first example, a person who has a bad headache and is visibly suffering; we surely want to say he *knows* that he is in pain. Yet it seems out of place to say to him: "So you believe you're in pain; what's your evidence?" or "What reasons do you have to offer in support of your belief that you're in pain?" or "What sort of a case can you make for the supposition that you're in pain?" The inappropriateness of such questions is apparent also in the case of feelings or moods: We do not expect a man to present evidence, even broadly construed, in support of his statement "I'm feeling sad today." Nor, finally, for the perceptual statement "The sky seems to me to be growing darker" do we suppose any need for the setting forth of a supporting case. Yet it seems undeniable that a man may *know* that he is feeling sad or that the sky seems to him to be growing darker. His *statements,* cited above, may normally be expressive rather than descriptive in function; yet, *that* he has the appropriate *knowledge* seems impossible to deny. In all these instances, nevertheless, there would seem to be no "logical room" for the concept of evidence to apply. Consequently, if someone *believes,* for example, that he is in pain (belief condition satisfied), and he is *really* in pain (truth condition satisfied), then he *knows that* he is in pain and no further condition of *evidence* seems to apply; a similar conclusion appears warranted also for feelings and for perceptual experiences.

It might be supposed that we have here another argument for the certainty of phenomenal statements, since, if the concept of evidence is indeed inapplicable, these statements are immune to criticism by analysis of their purportedly supporting evidence. Even if *such* immunity be admitted, however, it does not follow that the statements in question are immune from error; there may, in fact, be strong independent grounds for rejecting such statements, *initially* accepted without supporting argument. We have earlier noted (in the fourth section of the previous chapter) how competing beliefs may force revision in phenomenal judgments if the consistency of one's whole mass of beliefs is to be maintained. A single statement may be accepted as worthy of belief simply by virtue of its high prima facie credibility at the time and without attempt to build an evidential case for it. Nonetheless, it will still be subject to withdrawal on reasonable grounds through conflict with other statements having a higher combined prima facie credibility.[3]

Furthermore, it is misleading, at best, to say there is no "logical room" for the concept of evidence in the domain of phenomenal cases we have considered. For all these cases represented peculiarly "first-person" situations: We found it odd to ask someone for supporting reasons to back up his belief in *his own* headache; similarly, we found it odd to request evidence *from the speaker* in support of his utterance "I'm feeling sad" or "It seems to me the sky is growing darker." But, surely, another person might well be queried to the same effect, without oddness, in each of these cases. Such a person, a doctor, for example, may indeed be conceived to have good reasons in support of his judgment that a given patient has a headache or is feeling sad or is perceiving the sky as growing darker. Furthermore, there is nothing in the logic of the case to prevent the patient himself from stating, or restating, the doctor's reasons. It is, therefore, not that "evidence" is *logically inapplicable* in these cases, but rather that we do not here *require* the person to offer evidence in order to be said by us to *know*.

Under certain conditions, we grant that he is in a *position to* know, that he does not normally *need* to piece together clues and process them by some preferred method of inquiry. Now where such a method *is* thought to be normally needed, we are concerned to distinguish those cases where it is correctly applied from those cases where the right conclusion is gotten accidentally, as, for example, by lucky guessing. We will want the doctor to have based his judgment of the patient's pain upon accepted methods of interpreting diagnostic clues, and not simply to have made a lucky guess. But the patient's position and the doctor's position are asymmetrical with respect to the patient's pain. We typically suppose that the patient is in a position to decide relatively "directly" about his own pain, that a statement about his pain may thus have an initially high prima facie credibility for the patient, though not for his doctor. We therefore grant the patient the *right* to decide relatively "directly" the question of his own pain, and if he is right, we acknowledge that he knows. Since we do not require him, further, to follow some general method, there is no question of trying to eliminate the possibility of his short-circuiting such a method through lucky guessing. Nor is a person's right to decide relatively "directly" limited to statements about his own pains, moods, and perceptual experiences. The issue is much broader than phenomenalism. If he says his name is *Robert,* we do not, outside of legal contexts, think it appropriate to ask him for a statement of the evidence, nor do we marvel at his lucky guess if, though he follows no general method of decision, he nonetheless comes up with the right answer. If he is looking out the window and says, "The postman is coming up the walk," we do not think to ask, "What's your evidence?"

It is important to be clear that, in not requiring a supporting case, we are *not* granting immunity from error. In every example we have referred to, error is possible, and infallibility therefore ruled out. A man may be mistaken even about his own name, or his own pains or moods, in circumstances that may be unusual but are nonetheless readily imagined. What we *are* doing is granting the right to decide certain questions on the basis of high prima facie credibility and without evidential argument in a variety of cases of propositional knowledge. In these cases, we are saying, in effect, that it is enough that the person is in a *position* to know; we are granting that his position is so authoritative with respect to the belief in question that if he believes truly, he knows.

It would seem, then, that the evidence condition is too strong a general requirement for propositional knowledge. For in such cases as we have lately considered, a person may indeed know that *Q* without having adequate evidence that *Q.* Yet, if the evidence condition is too strong, we still need some general way of characterizing the surplus force of *knowing* over *believing truly.* We need, in short, to formulate some weaker, more abstract condition than the evidence condition, that will embrace all those cases where *evidence* is required, as well as all those cases in which being in a *position* to know is itself sufficient.

J. L. Austin's work suggests the idea of *authority* or *right* as relevant in this connection. Austin draws an analogy between certain features of epistemological language and certain aspects of legal or moral language. Consider promising, for example. If a person says "I promise to return the book by next Tuesday," his statement does not *describe* his promising to return the book. Rather, his very statement *constitutes* his promising. In Austin's terminology, his statement is *performative* rather than *descriptive.* It does not describe, but rather *is,* an act—in this case, an act associated with the main verb of the sentence. This act may, for example, be *described* by means of this verb in the third person, e.g., "He promises to return the book." The original first-person statement, however, does not describe something *else* which is the promise, but *itself* constitutes the promise in question. Saying "I promise," under the proper circumstances, creates an obligation for the speaker and a corresponding right for

the person to whom the promise is made. In this respect, it is quali-
tatively different from saying even "I fully intend to," for the latter
creates no such obligation or right.

> When I say "I promise" [writes Austin] a new plunge is
> taken: I have not merely announced my intention, but, by
> using this formula (performing this ritual), I have bound
> myself to others, and staked my reputation, in a new way.
> Similarly, saying "I know" is taking a new plunge. But it
> is *not* saying "I have performed a specially striking feat of
> cognition, superior, in the same scale as believing and being
> sure, even to being merely quite sure": for there *is* nothing
> in that scale superior to being quite sure. Just as promising
> is not something superior, in the same scale as hoping and
> intending, even to merely fully intending: for there *is* nothing
> in that scale superior to fully intending. When I say "I know,"
> I *give others my word: I give others my authority for saying* that
> "S is P" (p. 67).[4]

Austin's account is somewhat misleading. Clearly, he cannot
mean to say that the utterance of "I know" in proper circumstances
is the knowing, as the utterance of "I promise" in proper circumstances *is* the promising. His essential point is rather the following:
Just as the surplus force of "I promise" over "I fully intend" is
not to describe but rather to obligate or bind in special ways, so
the surplus force of "I know" over "I am quite sure" is not to
describe but rather to obligate or bind in special ways. "I know"
operates, in other words, as a conventionalized act, to create special
bonds. The following quotation from Austin is worth citing in full:

> When I have said only that I am sure, and prove to have
> been mistaken, I am not liable to be rounded on by others
> in the same way as when I have said "I know". I am sure
> *for my part*, you can take it or leave it: accept it if you think
> I'm an acute and careful person, that's your responsibility.
> But I don't know "for my part", and when I say "I know"
> I don't mean you can take it or leave it (though of course
> you *can* take it or leave it). In the same way, when I say I
> fully intend to, I do so for my part, and according as you
> think highly or poorly of my resolution and chances, you will
> elect to act on it or not to act on it: but if I say I promise,
> you are *entitled* to act on it, whether or not you choose to do
> so. If I have said I know or I promise, you insult me in a
> special way by refusing to accept it. We all feel the very great
> difference between saying even "I'm *absolutely* sure" and saying

"I know": it is like the difference between saying even "I firmly and irrevocably intend" and "I promise" (p. 68).

The saying of "I know" is taken to involve a claim of authority to make the substantive assertion in question, and a transfer of such authority to others, by which they acquire the right to bank on the assertion, the speaker accepting all responsibility if it turns out mistaken. Now Austin is concerned with the performative force of the first-person "I know," and he does not address himself particularly to the third-person descriptive "He knows." But, clearly, to say "He knows" is *not* to affirm that he has uttered the performative "I know," or some equivalent. In this respect, as we have earlier intimated, the parallel with promising is misleading, for "He promises" does lend itself to such an interpretation. In the case of knowing, by contrast, we may be prepared to say "He knows" even where he has never *said* "I know" or anything comparable.

Furthermore, even where he *has* said "I know," effectively asserting his authority for the claim in question and accepting full responsibility for it, we may still ask whether he does indeed have the authority he asserts. To say he knows is thus not merely (or even) to acknowledge that he has effectively bound himself by *pledging his word;* it is to affirm rather that he has the *proper authority* for the item in question, *the right* to make a relevant claim, without qualification.

A. J. Ayer suggests, in this connection, the notion "having the right to be sure."[5] In the third-person descriptive cases we are now concerned with—that is, in judging whether or not X knows that Q—we need to decide whether X has the *right* to be sure that Q, not whether he has said "I know that Q." The utterance of "I know" by X may be admitted to have the performative force Austin describes; it may indeed be a special formula for assigning rights and accepting responsibility by pledging one's word. Nonetheless, it may be independently asked whether X does in fact know. To say that *he* does is for *us* to admit that his possible claim to authority is *legitimate;* it is to affirm his *right* to be sure. This formulation of Ayer's, building on Austin's epistemological use of the language of authority and rights, seems a likely candidate for the wanted successor to the evidence condition.

For the right to be sure is, indeed, a more abstract and more comprehensive condition than the evidence condition. It can readily be conceived as covering those cases where evidence is required as a condition of knowing, as well as those cases where it is not. In fact, it is useful in the present connection just because *rights* are typically distinguished from the *circumstances* under which they are granted. These circumstances may vary with the situation in question, and they are, moreover, subject to revision over time, with new knowledge or changing purposes. There is thus no difficulty in supposing that the right to be sure, in particular, is granted under circumstances that may vary with subject-matter, standards of rigor, and educational purposes. In any event, the normative or appraisal function of knowledge attributions, earlier stressed, holds equally under the present interpretation.

There is, however, one difficulty with the "right to be sure" condition that needs to be met. Generally, to do something which one has no right to do carries an implication of blame; one ought not to do what one has no right to do. Accordingly, then, one is subject to blame in being sure when one has no right to be sure. But this implication of blame is not generally appropriate in questions of knowledge assessment. If a child does not know that Q, because, although he is sure, he does not yet have adequate grounds for his belief, we do not always blame him. It may be that it is just the appropriate standards of adequacy that he has yet to learn and that we are trying, at the moment, to teach him. Before he has learned these standards, he incurs no blame for being sure without sufficient grounds. To say he has no right to be sure of "Q" gives the wrong impression that in his being sure, he has done something generally blameworthy. Analogously, we may well want to say of a thinker in some earlier age or simple culture that his grounds for a particular belief are inadequate, without thereby blaming him for his assurance with respect to that belief. In *his* circumstances, it may well be that his assurance is not blameworthy, since he has had no motivation or reasonable basis for the more rigorous standards by which we judge.

It is, thus, important explicitly to distinguish the question of the *adequate grounding of a belief* from the question of *appraisal of the believer.* Just as it is important to separate the appraisal of an *action* (in terms of its objective consequences) from appraisal of the *agent's acting* (in terms of its relevant motives and intended consequences), so we need to separate the appraisal of a *belief* (in terms of its credentials) from appraisal of a given person's *believing* (in terms of its background and circumstances).

To speak of the right to be sure is, in the present context, to appraise the *credentials* of belief from the vantage point of our own standards; it is to spell out the attitude of these standards toward specific *credentials* offered for a belief. It does not also give us an automatic judgment of the *believer;* in particular, it does not support an imputation of blame for violation of our standards in given circumstances. In the same vein, we may speak of rights, generally, from the point of view of our code of law, without implying that any agent's action in violating our code is blameworthy. In short, the "right to be sure" condition requires what may be called an *objective interpretation* if it is to be free from difficulty, and we shall suppose such an interpretation henceforth.

We now replace the original evidence condition by the condition: "*X* has the right to be sure that *Q*." Our original sample definition will now read:

X knows that Q

if and only if

(i) X believes that Q,
(ii) X has the right to be sure that Q,
and   (iii) Q.

SUBJECTIVE CERTAINTY AND THE TIMID STUDENT

With our new "right to be sure" condition, should not the belief condition be changed also, to require that X be sure of "Q"? There is a certain naturalness to this idea: knowing would involve *being* sure when it is *legitimate* to be sure, it would imply exercising one's right to be sure. We would, following such a proposal, be requiring certainty in a *purely subjective* sense, compatible with the rejection of all claims to objective certainty or infallibility. Ayer indeed takes this course, asserting "that the necessary and sufficient conditions for knowing that something is the case are first that what one is said to know be true, secondly that one be sure of it, and thirdly that one should have the right to be sure."[6]

This requirement of "subjective certainty" is possible to stipulate, of course, but it is not forced upon us simply by adoption of the "right to be sure" condition. Furthermore, there are certain considerations that militate against requiring even subjective certainty for knowledge, especially in educational contexts. We may present these considerations by referring to the *case of the timid student:* It may be desirable to admit that such a student *knows* that Q, although he lacks *strong conviction* that Q. The student may, for example, be generally lacking in self-confidence, or he may have a history of poor work in related subjects, or he may have had some bad experience in the course of learning that Q. Any number of circumstances may account for his timidity. Nonetheless, he may have grasped the essentials of the subject and fully mastered its techniques. The timid student may not, himself, say "I know"; he may offer his uniformly correct answers or solutions with considerable diffidence. Yet we may feel strongly inclined to assure him that he does, in fact, know, that he has, in point of fact, the right to be surer than he is.

In accordance with such an approach, we would take knowing to imply not the *exercise* of one's right to be sure but only the *possession* of this right; as elsewhere, so here too, a person clearly may have rights he is not exercising nor is even aware of having. The timid student, in particular, may need to be encouraged to exercise his legitimate right to be sure. To allow that he nevertheless *knows* is, in effect, to distinguish him from the student who is ignorant of the proposition in question or of its proper grounds, and who, for this reason, does not know.

The ignorant or untutored student requires to be given arguments or evidence by the teacher, or at least to be afforded the opportunity to acquire such evidence or develop such arguments in connection with the proposition in question. This is one sort of thing the teacher is typically called upon to do. The timid student, on the other hand, does not require this, for he has already learned the proposition as well as its relevant backing and associated techniques. He rather requires encouragement and whatever other treatment may be desirable in bolstering his security and self-assurance with respect to the topic in question. This is another, and quite different, thing the teacher may be expected to do. One virtue of leaving the belief condition as it was and not requiring subjective certainty is that this distinction remains clearly marked. We shall thus *not* strengthen the belief condition to require that X be *sure* that Q; we shall hold it enough that he *believes* that Q, no matter what the degree of his subjective certainty.

THE POSSESSION OF ADEQUATE EVIDENCE

We have substituted the "right to be sure" condition for the original evidence condition because the latter seemed too stringent as a general requirement. The former, on the other hand, we considered to have the advantage of covering those cases of propositional knowledge where evidence is required, as well as those cases where it is not. Consider now just the former cases: In the second section of the present chapter, we raised certain questions concerning the *adequacy* of evidence. We now ask: "What does it mean to *have* adequate evidence?"

In our earlier discussion in the second section, we required X's total evidence to be adequate, and we acknowledged that standards of adequacy vary with context. Here we shall address ourselves to the interpretation of X's *having* evidence which adequately supports "Q," assuming that the evidence in question is either the totality of X's evidence, or that segment of the totality which is relevant to "Q," and assuming also that our operative standards of adequacy are fixed in context.

One small but important digression which concerns the fixing of our standards of adequate evidence is here worth making. Earlier, we referred primarily to the question of *leniency or stringency* in applying such standards in given contexts. It is now important to note that the classroom situation typically imposes also *qualitative* restrictions to certain *sorts* of evidence. Suppose, for example, that the student is to find the answer to an arithmetic problem. He looks at his friend's paper; knowing him to be reliable in arithmetic matters, he copies his answer, which happens to be right. Or, suppose the student believes truly that the answer is 748 because he recalls the teacher's saying so when the problem had been earlier considered in class, his evidence for the truth of his belief including also the fact that the teacher has been generally trustworthy on arithmetical topics. Does the student then not have the right to be sure; does he not then know? It would seem that the answer is affirmative; yet, if he offers such evidence in justification of his answer, it will be rejected.

The basis for such rejection, it may be thought, is the fact that the student's evidential case consists in an appeal to authority. Augustine, as we have seen, indeed holds that such an appeal can yield only belief, not knowledge. On this view, the "right to be sure" condition and the evidence condition are both too weak, since they admit arguments from authority. This view seems, however, itself too severe. We should all, for example, commonly be admitted to know that penicillin is helpful in cases of pneumonia, that there are consistent non-Euclidean geometries, that Washington was the first President of the United States, and that coffee is grown in Brazil even though our evidence for these items consists, for the most part, in an appeal to authority or the testimony of expert opinion. In the case of the student we have considered, we should, in fact, grant *outside the classroom* that he *does* know the answer to his problem, having based himself on a reasonable appeal to authority. What seems to be involved here is thus not a blanket exclusion of such appeals but rather a special requirement of the classroom context.

Inside the classroom, we want the boy to provide not an appeal to authority, no matter how reasonable and how strong; we want him rather to supply evidence from within the subject at hand. We want to determine not simply whether he *knows* the answer, but whether he knows it on, for example, arithmetical grounds. He is expected, in the classroom, to appeal to the authority of the relevant methods and materials of his subject rather than to the independent authority of persons. We must, to be sure, avoid a sharp distinction in the present context between personal authority and direct substantive evidence, for the subject itself may incorporate methodologically sanctioned appeals to personal authority, e.g., the authority of testimony in history or the authority of scientific reports. But we have, nevertheless, a contrast between the sort of evidence integral to the subject being taught and authoritative appeals that are extraneous to the subject. Operative standards of adequacy within the classroom will normally be restricted to evidence of the first sort, and *knowing in classroom contexts* will accordingly be more narrowly interpreted than *knowing in everyday life,* our educational purpose being, after all, to interiorize the subject—its methodology as well as its content—within the student.

Turning now to our main question, the *possession* of adequate evidence, we shall henceforth presuppose the special restrictions of the classroom situation and allow only evidence integral to the subject itself. Let us consider first a geometrical example, employing our previously expanded sense of *evidence,* which includes proofs.

A boy knows the axioms and rules of Euclidean geometry and, further, believes truly that a certain sentence S is a theorem in this geometry. Does he have adequate evidence, and does he therefore know, that S is a Euclidean theorem? It might be suggested that he literally has the strongest possible evidence that S is a Euclidean theorem, for he has *all* the requisite materials for a deductive proof of S within Euclidean geometry. Still, to have all the materials for a deductive proof is not yet to have adequate evidence; the boy may know the axioms and rules and still merely have guessed that S is a theorem. Should he, in particular, lack a proof of S, he could hardly be said to have the right to be sure that S is a theorem. Though the axioms and the rules are adequate for the proof of S, and though the boy possesses the axioms and the rules, he does not yet possess adequate evidence that S is a theorem. Is there a contradiction here? Not so. We just need to recognize that having adequate evidence for a given statement is not simply having materials adequate for the demonstration of that statement.

Finding a demonstration is, in general, *not* a routine process, even though *checking* a demonstration, once found, *is* routine.[7] Since finding a demonstration is rather a matter of ingenuity and luck— a "creative" outcome rather than a methodical application of rule to available items—possession of rule and items is clearly weaker than having a demonstration: not only is it itself no proof, but it does not routinely or mechanically yield a proof, even where such a proof exists. We thus plausibly differentiate having adequate evidence, in the form of an actual proof, from having merely the rules and items adequate to support a proof. We ask, in short, that the rules and items be organized and elaborated into an appropriate proof pattern. Having adequate evidence for "Q" is not, in general, simply having materials adequate to yield "Q"; the proper *pattern* of argument must also be "had."

When we turn from mathematical to ordinary empirical cases, the same conclusion seems inescapable. Consider a typical situation in a detective story: The detective, at a certain point in the development of the plot, has all the clues and, furthermore, has the correct hunch that the butler is the culprit. Yet, he does not *know*—that is, have the right to be sure. What is missing? We do not, in this situation, expect or require a deductive proof, but we do need some patterning of the clues, some *evidential argument*, in short, lending reasonable warrant to the detective's conclusion.

Typically, we expect a theoretical reconstruction of the crime, differentially supported by the relevant evidence and implicating the butler while ruling out the other suspects. Short of some such evidential argument by the detective, how can he have the right to be sure of his suspicions regarding the butler? From our standpoint, how do we know, unless we have reason to suppose such an argument available to the detective, that he has indeed appreciated the force of the clues he has, or has even "seen them as" clues? In empirical cases such as these, the pattern of argument is surely not mechanically derivable from the clues, even when they are recognized to be clues; theoretical ingenuity comes into play. Again, clearly, to *have* adequate evidence is not simply a matter of having evidence which is adequate to support an appropriate argument; it is to have such an argument as well.

Having evidence is, moreover, itself ambiguous. We have been stressing the importance of creative argument, which goes beyond the having of evidential clues. But it is worth distinguishing two senses in which one may be said merely to have such evidential clues. In the stronger sense, this involves the realization that such items constitute evidence, though their bearing may as yet not be clearly apprehended. In the weaker sense, having the clues does not even require the realization that they constitute evidence; the evidential items are "had" in some rudimentary way but are as yet camouflaged, not neatly sifted and separated as relevant elements for an appropriate argument, nor even appreciated as having potential value for some such argument. At a critical point in the development of the typical detective story, the reader is informed that he now has all the clues available to the detective hero, indeed all the evidence needed for the solution of the crime. Obviously, the sense in which the reader has the evidence is one which does not imply that he has recognized the evidential items as such, much less used them to provide differential support for a theoretical reconstruction of the crime. Such a theoretical reconstruction is thus "doubly" creative in comparison with the reader's situation: it not merely *singles out the clues as relevant* from the mass of environmental camouflage, but patterns them into an appropriate argument. There is no mechanical routine which is capable of this sort of theorizing. Furthermore, the situation of the reader is just the typical situation of the detective himself at an earlier stage and, more importantly, of the mathematician seeking a proof and the scientist seeking a theory of nature. In every case where evidence is required for the right to be sure, knowing involves not merely having adequate evidential data but also appreciating their value *as* data, in the light of an appropriately patterned *argument*.

But what is it now to *have* such an *argument?* Is having such an argument simply having the capacity to reproduce it? Suppose a boy has seen a mathematical proof somewhere, without being able to recall the source. He can, however, reproduce it. Has he fulfilled the requirements of the evidence condition? Certainly he must do more than produce an accurate physical replica of the original proof he has seen; he must *understand* the proof, *see its point*.

It is not, however, easy to say how such understanding is itself to be characterized. Surely, the boy needs to understand the language in which the proof is couched, but this does not seem to be enough. We can all recall experiences in which we have read through genuine proofs or valid arguments in familiar language without having understood them. To hark back to detective stories again, has not every reader had the experience of failing to grasp the detective's long-awaited explanation after having read it through for the first time? Yet what is missing, in such cases, that further reading or explanation can supply?

Perhaps we can say this: One may appreciate the *force* of an argument—that is, one may see the general import of the reasons behind its conclusion and may, further, attain a grasp of the general strategy that gives it unity. For is it not, again, a common experience to have grasped the rule governing each step in an argument and yet to have felt that one had missed the full point? Perhaps it is indeed too strong a *requirement* to ask for an appreciation of *strategy* as well as for a grasp of the *rules* governing each link in the chain of argument. Here we are concerned, however, just to spell out what factors may be involved in seeing the point of a proof. The requirement may be set independently.

Henri Poincaré has discussed certain related issues in his essay "Mathematical Definitions and Education."[8] He asks, "Does understanding the demonstration of a theorem consist in examining each of the syllogisms of which it is composed in succession, and being convinced that it is correct and conforms to the rules of the game?" (p. 118) For some people, he thinks that such a procedure suffices. "But not," he goes on, "for the majority."

Almost all are more exacting: they want to know not only

whether all the syllogisms of a demonstration are correct, but why they are linked together in one order rather than in another. As long as they appear to them engendered by caprice, and not by an intelligence constantly conscious of the end to be attained, they do not think they have understood. No doubt they are not themselves fully aware of what they require and could not formulate their desire, but if they do not obtain satisfaction, they feel vaguely that something is wanting. Then what happens? At first they still perceive the evidences that are placed before their eyes, but, as they are connected by too attenuated a thread with those that precede and those that follow, they pass without leaving a trace in their brains, and are immediately forgotten; illuminated for a moment, they relapse at once into an eternal night. As they advance further, they will no longer see even this ephemeral light, because the theorems depend one upon another, and those they require have been forgotten. Thus it is that they become incapable of understanding mathematics (pp. 118–119).

Poincaré suggests the importance, for certain minds, of having a unifying image, and he further stresses the role of intuition in giving a sense of the whole of a mathematical proof. He urges the importance of respecting the initial (faulty) images and intuitions of students in the process of mathematical education. If we reject these images and intuitions prematurely and force upon the students our superior formal constructions resting upon premises that

seem to them less evident than the conclusion, what will the wretched pupils think? They will think that the science of mathematics is nothing but an arbitrary aggregation of useless subtleties; or they will lose their taste for it; or else they will look upon it as an amusing game, and arrive at a state of mind analogous to that of the Greek sophists (p. 128).

Poincaré counsels initial encouragement of the pupils' intuitions and images so that, working with them, the pupils will begin to realize their inadequacies of themselves, at which point our formal demonstrations will be welcome and beneficial.

As methodological counsel to the teacher, Poincaré's advice seems plausible enough, yet he goes further than this in arguing that intuition is necessary for the pure mathematician himself.

Logic teaches us that on such and such a road we are sure of not meeting an obstacle; it does not tell us which is the road that leads to the desired end. For this it is necessary to see the end from afar, and the faculty which teaches us to see is intuition. Without it, the geometrician would be like a writer well up in grammar but destitute of ideas. Now how is this faculty to develop, if, as soon as it shows itself, it is hounded out and proscribed, if we learn to distrust it before we know what good can be got from it? (pp. 129–130)

Several points are worth notice in Poincaré's discussion. He suggests not only that imagination and intuition underlie the sense of the unity of a proof, but also that intuition is the source of mathematical discovery, for the sake of which we must, as teachers, be tactful in criticizing the intuitive constructions of our pupils. Nonetheless, he seems to contradict himself in admitting that the striving for images is characteristic of only certain, but not all, minds and in acknowledging that, even for creative mathematicians themselves, "We have only to read their works to distinguish among them two kinds of minds—logicians like Weierstrass, for instance, and intuitionists like Riemann" (p. 120). If nonintuitionistic minds among the mathematicians have a sense of unity of proofs and are capable, moreover, of high inventiveness, then clearly the faculty of *intuition* will not provide the requisite explanation.

Yet Poincaré seems certainly right in saying that understanding involves an *appreciation of the whole* of an argument and in attempting to link such appreciation somehow with inventiveness or discovery. Perhaps we can illuminate this difficult problem somewhat by considering first the single step in an argument and then the whole strategy which the argument represents. We remarked earlier that the general import of the reasons for the conclusion must be seen; what this means for the single step is that the pupil must possess the *general principle* which characterizes the relevant item as a reason. And this further means that he must have a general ability to recognize *comparable* reasons in *analogous* arguments elsewhere. Indeed, to have the general principle does not imply that it can be *stated* but only that a specific reason falling under its scope can be judged similar in its justifying force to analogous reasons elsewhere. Reasons and principles are conjugate notions, and understanding is thus inherently *general;* to understand a single step is to understand an indefinitely large number of comparable steps.

How, indeed, do we in practice judge if a boy has seen the point of a given step? We normally test to see if he can apply or discern the same form of reasoning in other cases. We ask him to innovate, or at least to recognize the same sort of reasoning elsewhere. Such confrontation with other, new cases at one and the same time *tests* and *develops* the requisite understanding of the pupil.

Further, it leads him into fresh and untried situations and encourages him to note analogies and to take risks in making guesses at underlying principles; this is surely a desirable, if not a sufficient, sort of training for discovery. Turning now to the whole *strategy* of an argument, "seeing the end from afar," as Poincaré so aptly puts it, we have here not a justifying principle for an inferential step but something more in the nature of a *motive*. To grasp the strategy is to see what end the author of the argument hoped to achieve at the outset *and* by what major means he hoped to achieve it. His strategy justifies not his step-by-step inferences but his choice of direction; it is not a reason for any particular step, in the sense of a governing or validating principle; it is rather a reason why he starts where he does and marshals his principles in such wise as to move here rather than there. Knowing his strategy, we know what long-term goal motivates him, what he foresees as the immediate outcome of his present step, and why he supposes this outcome to bring him closer to the sought goal.

Though strategies are not justifying principles of inferences, they do justify choices of direction and they are, like principles, general in having embodiments in a variety of cases. Thus, to tell if a student has appreciated a particular strategy, we can, as before, test to determine if he recognizes analogous strategies elsewhere or can innovate in stragetically analogous ways. As before, too, strategic understanding may be developed concurrently with this process of testing, and the habit of looking at fresh situations with considerations of strategy in mind may be encouraged at the same time. The latter habit is surely a desirable condition from the point of view of an interest in discovery.

Actual discovery cannot be demanded as a condition for understanding, however, even though it constitutes strong evidence, when it occurs, of having understood the embodied strategy. Following an argument is easier than discovering it, and it would be absurd to suppose that no one understood Einstein who could not reproduce his discoveries. It is sufficient for understanding that the general force of the strategy be appreciated, that its embodiments in other, perhaps simplified and hypothetical cases, be recognized. If this analysis is correct, then having adequate evidence involves, in any event, a generalized sort of ability—namely, the ability to deal appropriately with new cases beyond the one under consideration.

Strategies and principles are, we have suggested, ways of patterning data into arguments. They do not, however, constitute self-sufficient mechanisms of discovery. A basic problem in teaching is how to transmit our arguments, principles, and strategies without closing off fruitful *innovations* we have not ourselves anticipated. We need to avoid conducting our teaching as if all educative roads lead to our accepted patterns.

To summarize, when we judge that someone has adequate evidence, we are judging that he has an evidential argument which he understands. In saying he knows, we are not merely ascribing true belief but asserting that he has proper credentials for such belief, the *force* of which he himself *appreciates*. We are thereby certifying certain general abilities that carry over to other situations and that are most clearly evidenced in innovation.

•

CHAPTER FOUR

Knowledge and Belief

•

THE PROBLEM OF INTERPRETING BELIEF

We turn now to the remaining condition of our sample definition of propositional knowledge: the *belief condition*. This condition stipulates that if X knows that Q, he believes that Q.

Let us recall some of the points that emerged out of our discussion of the performative use of *know* (in the third section of Chapter III). We noted that such use is peculiar to the first person and that the third person "He knows" does not simply report the performative "I know." Analogously, the third person "He believes" does not simply report the first person "I believe," which frequently has the special force of disclaiming the authority of *knowledge*, or denying subjective *certainty*. Thus, a person may *in fact* believe that Q, although he actively refrains from *saying* "I believe." Though the *uttering* of "I believe" would tend to convey the speaker's lack of knowledge, his *actual belief* is perfectly compatible with his knowledge. The belief condition thus involves no inconsistency in holding that X (actually) believes that Q, if he knows that Q. We must avoid confusing actual belief with the utterance of "I believe."

But what are we attributing to X in describing him as actually believing that Q? What sort of thing is belief? These questions touch on some of the most perplexing problems in the theory of knowledge. We may begin our present consideration of them by recalling Ryle's critique of the view of knowing as a mental performance (in the second section of Chapter II). We remarked that his arguments applied equally to believing. For example, to the question "What are you *doing*?" one could not well reply "Believing that it will rain tomorrow." Nor could one properly speak of being *engaged* in believing something at the moment, or of being *too busy* believing to accept an invitation to take a walk. The category of performance or activity indeed seems inappropriate for belief.

Nor does the notion of a special mental experience, act, or occurrence fare better, it would seem. We have all believed firmly for a long time that $3 \times 6 = 18$. But no one has had a continuous series of distinctive mental acts or experiences associated with this belief, starting with the moment it was first learned. It seems surely more plausible to construe belief as a relatively abstract *state*, but how, in detail, shall we interpret such a construal?

The problem may be illustrated by referring to Peirce's contrast of doubt and belief. Peirce stressed the qualitative difference between the two, doubt being "an uneasy and dissatisfied state from which we struggle to free ourselves and pass into the state of belief," the latter itself being "a calm and satisfactory state which we do not wish to avoid" (p. 99). Doubt is a specific stimulus and "reminds us of the irritation of a nerve and the reflex action produced thereby," whereas "belief does not make us act at once, but puts us into such a condition that we shall behave in a certain way, when the occasion arises." Rather than an analogy with a nerve irritation, we need, in the case of belief, to "look to what are called nervous associations— for example, to that habit of the nerves in consequence of which the smell of a peach will make the mouth water" (p. 99).

Belief is, then, let us suppose, an abstract thing, in the nature of a habit or readiness, a disposition to act in certain ways under certain circumstances. But—and here is our problem—*what* ways and *what* circumstances? The reference to an association connecting the smell of a peach with the mouth's watering is delightfully specific both as to the condition and the response which are joined together. Can anything comparably specific be said in the case of belief, on the assumption that it, too, is an association of response with circumstance?

THE VERBAL THEORY OF BELIEF AND ITS DIFFICULTIES

In answer to the question just posed, many writers have suggested what may be called a "verbal theory" of belief. We shall consider some variants of this (perhaps predominant) theory.

We turn first to R. Carnap's account.[1] Carnap suggests, for the sentence:

(i) John believes that *D*,

the analysis: (ii) John is disposed to an affirmative response to some sentence in some language, which is a close translation of *"D."*

This is not Carnap's actual wording, but we may, for our present purposes, abstract from several technicalities of his treatment. The main idea may be put thus: *belief that D* is explained as affirmation of a close translation of *"D."* To say, for example:

>   (iii) John believes that algebra is diffi-
>   cult,
>
> is to say:
>
>   (iv) John is disposed to respond af-
>   firmatively to some sentence which
>   is a close translation of "Algebra
>   is difficult."

(The reference to translation in (iv) enables us to affirm (iii) even though John knows no English and thus does not affirm "Algebra is difficult" but rather the equivalent in his language.)

Belief is generally, then, a disposition to offer an affirmative response to certain sentences under appropriate conditions—for example, under systematic questioning.[2]

In the course of discussing the importance of principles in education, R. M. Hare suggests a comparable version of the verbal theory. "Without principles," he says, "most kinds of teaching are impossible, for what is taught is in most cases a principle. In particular, when we learn *to do* something, what we learn is always a principle."[3] Hare goes on to assimilate the learning of facts to this same model: "Even to learn or be taught a fact (like the names of the five rivers of the Punjab) is to learn how to answer a question; it is to learn the principle 'When asked "What are the names of the five rivers of the Punjab?" answer "The Jhelùm, the Chenab, etc."'"[4] Presumably, to have learned this fact—that is, to have acquired the requisite belief—is to have gotten the disposition to produce the relevant names upon request, or perhaps just the disposition to answer affirmatively to them, (the weaker requirement being closer to Carnap's view). In any event, belief is here too a disposition to make specified verbal responses under appropriate conditions, in particular, under questioning.

B. F. Skinner, in his book *Verbal Behavior,* seems to suggest a more moderate form of the verbal theory. He interprets communication of knowledge or facts as the process of making a new response (frequently verbal) available to the speaker. It would seem that, according to this view, believing a fact is often a matter of having some verbal response available, *the situation varying, however, from field to field.* "In the field of history," says Skinner, "the effect is almost exclusively a modification of the student's future *verbal* behavior."[5] Having acquired belief in a historical fact, the student has acquired a distinctive sort of verbal disposition; a new form of verbal response has been made available to him. Apparently, the form of response in question is the affirmation or formulation of the fact involved, upon request.

The verbal theory of belief, as we understand it here, construes belief as a disposition to make certain linguistic responses, typically under conditions of questioning. The theory undoubtedly has a degree of initial plausibility, but it also has difficulties, to which we now address ourselves.

One obvious difficulty is that the theory denies belief to animals and infants, since they lack the capacity to make linguistic responses. This is perhaps not fatal, since the question of belief in the latter cases is independently controversial. Moreover, the scope of the theory may, in any event, be deliberately restricted to ideally clear cases—namely, to beliefs of organisms *with* language.

Granted this restriction, however, we now confront much more difficult problems, pertaining to the interpretation of the dispositions allegedly involved. What is it to be *disposed* to affirm or to formulate a sentence? In believing that algebra is difficult, does John perhaps have simply the *capacity* to affirm some appropriate sentence under questioning? In having learned the names of the five rivers of the Punjab, has the student acquired simply the *capacity* to produce these names or to affirm them, upon request? Are we to say, in these instances, that the relevant verbal responses have literally *been made available* as new *capacities* of the learner?

Surely, such a construal is wrong. For simply to know the language and to be free of physical speech impediments is already to have the *capacity to affirm* (e.g., by saying "Yes") and the *capacity to produce* (i.e., to pronounce) any sentence of the language. Knowing English and physically able to speak, John already has the *capacity* to say "Yes" to "Is algebra difficult?" as well as to *every other* question; yet John surely does not believe everything that might be put to him in the form of a question. Able merely to pronounce the names of the five rivers of the Punjab, the student already has the *capacity* to produce these names as verbal responses; yet he may not *know* the names of these rivers, by any reasonable criterion.[6]

In the latter case, it will perhaps be said that he needs still the capacity to *recall* these names under appropriate circumstances of questioning. But if capacity to recall and to pronounce the names of the five rivers of the Punjab were all that were necessary for the relevant belief, then, since the student normally has the capacity to recall and pronounce many other sets of five names under identical circumstances of questioning, we should need to describe him as believing, for example, that the names of the five rivers of the Punjab are Genesis, Exodus, Leviticus, Numbers, and Deuteronomy.

Skinner's notion of making a new response *available,* and so increasing the "repertoire" of responses, seems to be a *capacity* notion. It has been criticized by N. Chomsky, as follows:

> When we train a rat to carry out some particular act, it makes sense to consider this a matter of adding a response to his repertoire. In the case of human communication, however, it is very difficult to attach any meaning to this terminology. If *A* imparts to *B* the information (new to *B*) that the railroads face collapse, in what sense can the response *The railroads face collapse* be said to be now, but not previously, available to *B*? Surely *B* could have said it before (not knowing whether it was true), and known that it was a sentence. . . . Nor is there any reason to assume that the response has increased in strength, whatever this means exactly (e.g. *B* may have no interest in the fact, or he may want it suppressed).[7]

Suppose, then, we now take the disposition to affirm or produce the relevant sentence not as a mere *capacity* but as an active *tendency* or positive *propensity* to make the appropriate verbal response under questioning. For example, if John believes that algebra is difficult, he has the definite *propensity* to say "Yes" (or some equivalent) in response to the question "Is algebra difficult?" (or some close translation in a language John understands). If he has learned the names of the five rivers of the Punjab, he has the *tendency,* and not merely the *capacity,* to respond by listing these names when he is asked to do so.

This proposal has certain clear advantages over the previous one, for possession of the requisite *propensities* is not guaranteed simply by a knowledge of the language, absence of physical impediments to response, and appropriate capacities of recall. Nevertheless, the present proposal faces severe difficulties of its own: *Believing something* is not the same as having the tendency to *express or affirm the belief* under questioning. Indeed we have earlier noted one general difference; one can build up a habit or propensity through practice, but one cannot practice believing something. (See the second section of Chapter I, and the second section of Chapter II.)

A person may, moreover, believe that Q and lack the propensity to affirm or express "Q" or any translation of it, under questioning; indeed, he may have the counter propensity to *avoid* such affirmation or expression. An obvious, but extreme, example is the case of a spy in an enemy country, whose propensities to verbal response under questioning are systematically divergent from his genuine beliefs, at least on matters affecting his mission and his personal security. There are, moreover, numerous less extreme examples of the same sort of divergence. For one's propensities to verbal response under questioning are dependent not simply on belief but on independent factors of motivation and social climate. The avoidance of affirmation or expression of one's beliefs may, for instance, be motivated by fear, or rebelliousness, or embarrassment, or desire for approval. A child's lack of certain verbal propensities may thus represent, in given cases, not lack of the relevant beliefs but verbal *inhibitions* motivated by his fear of adults or his desire to win or maintain their approval.

Conversely, a person may have the active propensity to express or affirm some sentence, although he does not at all believe what it asserts. The examples already given need only be extended to provide clear cases of such contingencies. A spy in enemy territory does not merely refrain from revealing his genuine beliefs; he possesses strong propensities to make verbal responses which do not represent such beliefs. Systematic lying of more ordinary varieties is motivated often by fear, hostility, embarrassment, struggle for advantage, desire for approval, and so forth. The child's fear of adults, or endeavor to gain their approval, may induce not simply verbal inhibition but distortion—that is, the active propensity to say what he thinks will be approved by them, even if he does not believe it.

Students often acquire propensities to make those verbal responses to test questions that facilitate their passing their courses, or, at any rate, that are thought to reflect the attitudes and opinions of the test-makers, independently of their own genuine beliefs. Indeed, it is educationally of the utmost importance to avoid confusing genuine expression of belief with the production of what are considered expected test-responses. It is correspondingly important to distinguish the genuine engagement of students' thought and belief, in teaching, from the mere shaping of their verbal responses on examinations.

A final example is afforded by consideration of public opinion operating under political constraint of one or another sort. Such constraint in totalitarian systems, for example, serves not merely to inhibit the expression of "dangerous" beliefs but to foster active propensities to parrot the official line of political orthodoxy. Public expression of opinion in totalitarian countries thus provides no index of people's genuine beliefs. What is said under constraint is distorted by constraint. The support of public opinion often claimed for totalitarian systems can thus not be gauged simply by the unanimity of verbal propensities on public occasions—or even on private occasions—in societies dominated by political fear.

The verbal theory of belief thus seems to break down, whether we interpret the relevant dispositions as capacities or as tendencies. But perhaps, it may be suggested, the theory can be repaired in some way. Suppose, in particular, that we further circumscribe the conditions under which the verbal propensity is manifested: we do not stipulate merely a situation of questioning but build in certain additional specifications, to insure proper *motivation* by the person involved. For example, considering our earlier sentence:

> (iii) John believes that algebra is difficult,

we now analyze it as follows:

> (v) If John *decides* to respond to questions, he has the propensity *to respond* by affirming some sentence which is a close translation of "Algebra is difficult."

This analysis would clearly take care of some of the difficulties besetting the previous interpretation. It would not require, for every belief, a corresponding general propensity to affirm it under questioning. Thus, it would be consistent with at least some of those cases which we earlier described as involving *verbal inhibitions*, for in some such cases the necessary *decision to respond* was lacking, and thus the relevant affirming propensity did not need to be activated.

However, the analysis still breaks down in all those cases in which the person does indeed decide to respond under questioning but tends to affirm what he does not believe. The spy's trained responses to his captors provide a relevant counterexample here, as do those instances of systematic lying and other verbal distortions (e.g., responses under constraint) which were described earlier.

Perhaps, however, the activating conditions of the relevant verbal propensities need to be still further circumscribed. For all the latter counterexamples are cases where the decision to respond is not at the same time a decision to respond *truthfully*. Thus, let us propose for (iii) the following analysis:

> (vi) If John *decides to respond to questions truthfully*, he has the propensity to respond by affirming some sentence which is a close translation of "Algebra is difficult."

This analysis seems, at one stroke, to eliminate all the previous counterexamples, because in none of them was there a decision to respond *truthfully.* Thus neither verbal inhibition nor verbal distortion seems any longer to constitute a conclusive objection to the analysis proposed.

The question might, however, be raised as to whether the analysis is not, after all, *circular* in its present form. For what is John doing in deciding to respond *truthfully,* if he is not deciding to respond by saying what he truly *believes?* If so, the proposed analysis of belief itself appeals to the notion of belief, and the whole enterprise collapses in circularity.

This line of objection is not, however, really fatal to the proposal. For the precise form of the belief locution being analyzed does not itself recur in the analysis proposed, even when directly expressed in terms of *belief,* so there is, in fact, *no* explicit circularity: The sentence analyzed in our example was "John believes that algebra is difficult," and the form involved was thus: *"X believes that Q."* On the other hand, spelling out the analysis in terms of *belief,* as suggested in the previous paragraph, we should have "If John decides to respond to questions by saying what he truly believes, etc." This latter sentence contains rather the form *"X decides to respond by saying what he truly believes."* The latter form does not necessarily presuppose an interpretation for *"X* believes that *Q,"* to be expressed as some sort of function of *X* and *"Q."* It may be taken rather as representing a unitary condition characterizing *X* and qualifying his manner of response, i.e., his sincerity.

Furthermore, the term *belief* can be wholly eliminated from interpretation of the analysis expression. For deciding to respond truthfully can be taken simply as deciding to make the effort to say what is true. Belief that *Q,* is then analyzed as a propensity to respond to relevant questions by affirming some close translation of *"Q,"* given the decision to strive to say what is true in answer to such questions. (The latter decision, it may be assumed, could be ascertained, in a wide range of cases, without first determining the existence of the *belief that Q* itself.)

The proposal thus seems to escape the difficulty of circularity and also to avoid the earlier counterexamples of verbal inhibition and verbal distortion. There seem, however, to be new difficulties confronting this analysis. These arise from situations where inhibition or distortion take place even though the person does indeed genuinely strive to say what is true.

Expressing one's actual beliefs, to put the point briefly, is not dependent simply on the appropriate striving. A person may lack insight respecting his own beliefs. Or he may, through weakness of character or some other cause, develop a certain motivated blindness concerning certain beliefs of his, with respect to which he systematically deceives himself. In such circumstances, he may strive to say what is true but fail to express his beliefs accurately. Anyone who has ever sincerely asked himself, "What do I believe concerning such-and-such?", *not* in the sense "What ought I believe?" but rather in purely descriptive or introspective vein, realizes that the answering of this question requires deliberation and is by no means automatically protected from error simply by sincerity of intent.

Error often arises where a person cannot bring himself to acknowledge some belief which he has, but of which he reflectively disapproves or which he judges to be socially disapproved or even dangerous. Conversely, he may sincerely talk himself into profession of a belief which he does not really have "deep down," but which he reflectively approves or judges to be socially approved. An example of the first case is afforded by persons who really harbor vestiges of racist beliefs but sincerely deny having them. An example of the second case is provided by those who sincerely profess religious beliefs they do not really have. Accordingly, we sometimes describe people's sincere professions of belief as inaccurate or hollow; we judge that, in such cases, the person believes something else than what he says (or even thinks) he believes. Analogously, we occasionally refuse to take sincere denials of belief at face value. Considerations such as these count, moreover, not only against construing belief as a propensity to *overt* verbal response but also against construing belief as a propensity to "inner" verbal response, i.e., expression *to oneself*, or recall.

In typical circumstances we appeal to evidence beyond verbal response altogether, as to what a person's beliefs really are; we look to the way these beliefs are revealed in action. If we are prepared to acknowledge this point systematically, we must finally abandon the verbal theory of belief.

DIFFICULTIES IN THE GENERAL DISPOSITIONAL ACCOUNT

Peirce, it will be recalled, construes belief as dispositional; "belief . . . puts us into such a condition that we shall behave in a certain way, when the occasion arises" (p. 99). Believing that the stone is hard, the person is set to behave toward the stone in certain ways, should he wish to produce certain sensible results. The "habit of action" produced by thought leads one to act in certain ways "not merely under such circumstances as are likely to arise, but under such as might possibly occur, no matter now improbable they may be" (p. 123).

We have examined the verbal theory as an attempt to pin down the specific form of the disposition represented by belief, taking as a paradigm Peirce's reference to "that habit of the nerves in consequence of which the smell of a peach will make the mouth water" (p. 99). But in view of our criticism of the verbal theory, it would seem that Peirce's *general* description is closer to the mark than his particular example. If belief is dispositional, it must be a disposition not simply to this or that specific sort of response but to a variety of sorts of responses under a variety of conditions. It leads us to *act* in certain ways, and not merely to *talk* in certain ways.

Ryle emphasizes the importance of keeping in mind not only "single-track dispositions, the actualizations of which are nearly uniform" (p. 43),[8] but also "higher-grade dispositions" "the exercises of which are indefinitely heterogeneous" (p. 44). Single-track dispositions, in Ryle's sense, may be illustrated by the habit of pipe-smoking: "To be a smoker is just to be bound or likely to fill, light, and draw on a pipe in such and such conditions" (p. 43). Higher-grade dispositions are discussed by Ryle as follows:

> When Jane Austen wished to show the specific kind of pride which characterized the heroine of "Pride and Prejudice", she had to represent her actions, words, thoughts and feelings in a thousand different situations. There is no one standard type of action or reaction such that Jane Austen could say "My heroine's kind of pride was just the tendency to do this, whenever a situation of that sort arose" (p. 44).

Ryle goes on to criticize epistemologists who ascribe to knowing and believing "one-pattern intellectual processes in which these cognitive dispositions are actualized." He continues:

> Flouting the testimony of experience, they postulate that, for example, a man who believes that the earth is round must from time to time be going through some unique proceeding of cognizing, "judging", or internally re-asserting, with a feeling of confidence, "The earth is round". In fact, of course, people do not harp on statements in this way, and even if they did do so and even if we knew that they did, we still should not be satisfied that they believed that the earth was round, unless we also found them inferring, imagining, saying and doing a great number of other things as well. If we found them inferring, imagining, saying and doing these other things, we should be satisfied that they believed the earth to be round, even if we had the best reasons for thinking that they never internally harped on the original statement at all. However often and stoutly a skater avers to us or to himself, that the ice will bear, he shows that he has his qualms, if he keeps to the edge of the pond, calls his children away from the middle, keeps his eye on the life-belts or continually speculates what would happen, if the ice broke (pp. 44–45).

Ryle's reference to harping on statements is irrelevant for our purposes. For the verbal theory requires no such harping but only (at most) certain appropriate affirmation tendencies under restricted conditions of questioning. However, Ryle clearly asserts the thesis that belief dispositions may manifest themselves in all sorts of ways other than the affirmations stipulated by the verbal theory—e.g., in inferring, imagining, saying, and doing a variety of things. Furthermore, he clearly implies, in his example of the skater, that a man may be mistaken in gauging his own beliefs. For he pictures the skater as averring to himself that the ice will bear, while betraying in action that he believes no such thing, or at any rate that he has very serious reservations about it.

In another passage, Ryle seems to contradict himself while commenting on a comparable example. He writes,

> Certainly to believe that the ice is dangerously thin is to be unhesitant in telling oneself and others that it is thin, in acquiescing in other people's assertions to that effect, in objecting to statements to the contrary, in drawing consequences from the original proposition, and so forth. But it is also to be prone to skate warily, to shudder, to dwell in imagination on possible disasters and to warn other skaters. It is a propensity not only to make certain theoretical moves but also to make certain executive and imaginative moves, as well as to have certain feelings (pp. 134–135).

In the latter passage, he seems to make it a requirement of belief that the person be unhesitant in expressing it to himself, whereas in the earlier passage he allows that belief may be evident solely in action and that it may be at odds with one's own expressions to himself. It may, however, be that Ryle does not want to make expression of the belief a genuinely necessary condition in the latter passage, but only one among many typically associated symptoms of belief that would have to be judged as a totality; in any event, he denies it is a sufficient condition.

The broader dispositional view comes to this: A belief is a cluster of dispositions to do various things under various associated circumstances. The things done include responses and actions of many sorts and are not restricted to verbal affirmations. None of these dispositions is strictly necessary, or sufficient, for the belief in question; what is required is that a sufficient number of these clustered dispositions be present. Thus verbal dispositions, in particular, occupy no privileged position vis-à-vis belief.

This picture is, however, still not sufficiently broad, for we need to go beyond even the general description of belief as behavior dispositionally tied to occasion. This general description, while it does allow for *variety of response* and associated *variety of occasion* and is, moreover, *not restricted to verbal responses* alone, still seems to be too limited in other important respects.

Certainly, there are refinements to be effected in the construal of the dispositions themselves; they must, for example, be so interpreted as to embrace relatively loose probabilistic (and not only strictly universal) connections between occasion and response. But more important is the recognition that a man's beliefs hang together and exercise mutual influence upon one another, that they are, furthermore, in delicate interaction with his aims and attitudes. A single belief therefore cannot be attributed to a person simply on the basis of his response dispositions under given overt circumstances, no matter how varied these dispositions are taken to be. For the single belief is judged, in part, by reference to the other beliefs and the goals we assume the person to have; these other beliefs and goals color the circumstances under which the particular response is taking place. Relative to overt circumstances alone, therefore, we typically need to consider attributing a *complex* of beliefs and goals to the person. Since this complex is, moreover, underdetermined by his overt response dispositions, it is open to us to make the attribution in different ways, and we are influenced by considerations of overall simplicity in making our choice. Belief attribution, in short, looks more like abstract theoretical hypothesizing in the realm of science than like description of relatively low-level physical traits.

The complication thus effected in our view of belief goes beyond the general dispositional account given by Peirce and Ryle. Peirce indeed hints at the underlying point, but does not fully capitalize upon it. His pragmatic maxim, as we have seen, is intended to clarify general terms by construing them "operationally," i.e., as connecting certain sensible effects, dispositionally, to certain operations upon the object. The hardness of a thing is thus (or better, includes) its propensity to scratch certain test substances when it is rubbed against them. The sensible scratch is here tied to the overt, operational, occasion of rubbing. When Peirce turns to *belief,* he seems to be carrying out a parallel analysis in asserting that "the whole function of thought is to produce habits of action" (p. 123). For a *habit of action* is presumably the same sort of thing as the propensity or *habit of hardness* in the stone; it ties sensible responses to specific occasions of response. Peirce can thus conclude that "there is no distinction of meaning so fine as to consist in anything but a possible difference of practice" (p. 123).

Yet, earlier in the same paragraph, he elaborates on the occasions which activate a habit of action associated with a given belief, as follows: "What the habit is depends on *when* and *how* it causes us to act. As for the *when*, every stimulus to action is derived from perception; as for the *how*, every purpose of action is to produce some sensible result" (p. 123). And in the paragraph immediately following, he remarks, "The occasion of . . . action would be some sensible perception, the motive of it to produce some sensible result" (p. 123-124). Here, we see something new: the intrusion of references to *purpose* and *motive*, as well as to sensible perceptions. It is worth noting, in passing, that *another* person's sensible perceptions, i.e., what *he* perceives, is not an overt "sensible" matter from *our* point of view, concerned as we are to estimate *his* beliefs. More striking still is the element of *purpose or motive*, which Peirce introduces here but which he seems somewhat undecided as to how to treat. For in the first sentence quoted above, he clearly wants to make the belief habit dependent not only upon sensible stimulus *but also upon purpose*, while in the second sentence, he apparently wants to treat motive *not as belonging to the occasion itself* but as somehow constituting an independent factor qualifying the relevant response.

The factor of purpose or motive, however characterized, makes the whole account more plausible, to be sure. When a person believes that an object is hard, he is set to act toward it in certain ways, *provided* he has certain perceptions and *also* certain goals. To hark back to an example from the fifth section of Chapter II, should he *want* to make a mark upon some surface, he is set to use the stone as a marking instrument. However, the element of purpose or motive renders the whole account quite different from that of the hardness of the stone, for purpose is itself not an overt or "operational" matter, but as abstract and habitlike, and as much in need of "operational" clarification, as is belief itself. The general covering words *habit* and *occasion* suggest, in short, a parallelism which is not there, and the claimed reduction of belief to *practice* is thus without foundation.

THE THEORETICAL CHARACTER OF BELIEF ATTRIBUTIONS

Several fundamental points relevant to this issue have recently been brought out by C. G. Hempel, in a paper concerned with the concept of rational action.[9] Hempel introduces the term "broadly dispositional trait" to characterize rationality, but his treatment is also applicable to belief itself. A broadly dispositional trait involves a

> complex bundle of dispositions, each of them a tendency to behave in characteristic ways in certain kinds of situation (whose full specification would have to include information about the agent's objectives and beliefs, about other aspects of his psychological and biological state, about his environment, *et cetera*) (p. 13).

Hempel underscores the parenthesized point by stressing the contrast with relatively low-level traits such as allergic dispositions, for example. To say that a person "is allergic to ragweed pollen . . . is to imply, among other things, that he will exhibit the symptoms of a head cold when exposed to the pollen" (p. 14). In the case of *broadly dispositional traits*, by contrast, the relevant situations "cannot be described simply in terms of certain environmental conditions and external stimuli; for characteristically they include the agent's having certain objectives and entertaining certain relevant beliefs" (p. 14).

Hempel also maintains that attribution of a belief only implies, but is not equivalent to, a set of statements formulating "overt" dispositions of the person. He offers, as an analogy, the attribution of an electric charge to a physical object, which implies characteristic response dispositions but is not exhausted by them.

> For the concepts of electric charge, magnetization, and so on are governed by a network of theoretical principles interconnecting a large number of physical concepts. . . . the underlying theoretical assumptions contribute essentially to what is being asserted by the attribution of those physical properties. Indeed, it is only in conjunction with such theoretical background assumptions that a statement attributing an electric charge to a given body implies a set of dispositional statements; whereas the whole set of dispositional statements does not imply the statement about the charge, let alone the theoretical background principles (p. 15).

This proposed analogy with belief does not imply that there is a comparable degree of precision and explicitness in the interconnecting background assumptions. Nonetheless, Hempel argues that there are such "quasi-theoretical connections":

> For example, we assume that the overt behavior shown by a person pursuing a certain *objective* will depend on his beliefs; and conversely. Thus, the attribution, to Henry, of the belief that the streets are slushy will be taken to imply that he will put on galoshes only on suitable further assumptions about his objectives and indeed about his further beliefs; such as that he wants to go out, wants to keep his feet dry, believes that his galoshes will serve the purpose, does not feel in too much of a hurry to put them on, *et cetera:* and this plainly reflects the assumption of many complex interdependencies between the psychological concepts in question. It is these assumptions which determine our expectations as to what behavioral manifestations, including overt action, a psychological trait will

have in a particular case. . . . The point is . . . that to characterize the psychological features in question, we have to consider not only their dispositional implications, which provide operational criteria for attributing certain beliefs and objectives to a person: we must also take account of the quasi-theoretical assumptions connecting them; for these, too, govern the use of those concepts, and they cannot be regarded as logical consequences of the sets of dispositional statements associated with them (p. 15–16).

Finally, Hempel underscores the "epistemic interdependence" of *belief* attributions and *goal* attributions. We have quoted his example of this point in connection with Henry's *belief* that the streets are slushy, which implies that he will put on his galoshes, only on suitable assumptions about his goals. For *goals*, Hempel offers the complementary example of Henry's wanting a drink of water, which implies that he is "disposed to drink a liquid offered him—provided that he *believes* it to be potable water (and provided he has no overriding reasons for refusing to accept it, *et cetera*)" (p. 16). Hempel concludes, "Hence, strictly speaking, an examination of an agent's behavior cannot serve to test assumptions about his beliefs or about his objectives separately, but only in suitable pairs, as it were. . . ." (p. 16).

If this general view is correct, we cannot hope to pin belief down to specific overt response dispositions. We tentatively ascribe to persons clusters of beliefs and objectives in a way that is governed by general assumptions and considerations of simplicity not yet formulable with any great degree of explicitness. In practice, of course, the theoretical difficulties of formulation do not paralyze our judgment. As Hempel remarks,

> often we have good antecedent information about one of the interdependent items and then a hypothesis about the other may be tested by ascertaining how the person acts in certain situations. For example, we may have good grounds for the assumption that our man is subjectively honest; then his answers to our questions may afford a reliable indication of his beliefs. Conversely, we are often able to test a hypothesis about a person's objectives by examining his behavior in certain critical situations because we have good reasons to assume that he has certain relevant beliefs (pp. 16–17).

We may adopt the initial presumption of rationality, sincerity, and a sharing of common purposes. Then, with independent knowledge of the social context, we may judge belief as revealed in word and deed. Where these latter two diverge, we may need to decide whether to postulate weakness of will, or irrationality, or deviant purpose, or ignorance, or bizarre belief, or insincerity, and the choice may often be difficult. In any event, it will be affected by simplicity considerations and will be tentative in character. It will, in any case, never be reasonable to take belief simply as a matter of verbal response: belief is rather a "theoretical" state characterizing, in subtle ways, the orientation of the person in the world.

In the classroom, it seems particularly important to avoid mistaking verbal dispositions for belief. To this end, it is crucial that we recognize not only the ramifications of belief in conduct but also the influence of motivation and social climate on verbal expression. If we aim to engage the student's belief and not simply to shape his verbal output, we need to be able to *communicate* with him. For this to be possible, we need to create an atmosphere of security, so that verbal expression may approximate genuine belief. Such an atmosphere itself would seem to require an emphasis on rational discussion free of constraint and free of propagandistic tendencies: this emphasis underlies the common or standard sense of *teaching*.[10]

•

CHAPTER FIVE

Knowledge and Skill

•

PROPOSITIONAL KNOWLEDGE AND NORM STATEMENTS

We have spent the last three chapters discussing problems relating to propositional uses of *know*—i.e., cases of *knowing that*. We have anchored our discussions to a prevalent definition of *knowing that* requiring fulfillment of a belief condition, an evidence condition, and a truth condition. We have analyzed a variety of issues relating to each of these conditions, and offered interpretations of each, as well as a modification of the evidence condition itself. On the whole, our considerations have tended to support the prevalent definition which served us as a point of departure, although we did not consider general arguments to the effect that the definition fails to supply a sufficient condition of *knowing that*. Attributions of propositional knowledge do, in any case, seem (at least in the strong sense of *knowing that*) to involve as necessary conditions relevant assertions of belief, of truth, and of the possession of appropriate credentials for belief.[1]

Before turning to the procedural uses of *know* which are the proper concern of the present chapter, we shall deal briefly with one peculiar propositional case for which the prevalent definition might be thought insufficient, for special reasons. This is the case where the *knowing that* statement indicates a "norm," e.g., "*X* knows that he *ought* to be courteous to his classmates." In certain contexts, such a statement may be given an interpretation which may be termed "active."[2] Under this interpretation, the statement might appear to require a further condition beyond the three with which we have hitherto been concerned. For this interpretation requires that *X* incorporate the indicated norm in his own action—i.e., that he *be* courteous to his classmates: Where he fails to incorporate the norm in question, the present interpretation takes this as a clear indication that he does not *know* that he ought to be courteous to his classmates. On the active interpretation, in other words, if X has come to know that he ought to be courteous, he has learned to *be* courteous as a necessary condition, no matter what else may be involved. However, the prevalent definition seems to suffice if the belief condition itself is *also* given an active interpretation.

In any event, the active interpretation is not the only one available, and the weaker, *nonactive* interpretation drops the condition of norm-incorporation. The possible ambiguity as between active and nonactive interpretations is important, however, and I have elsewhere discussed some of its ramifications for concepts of learning and teaching.[3] In the present context we need merely note this potential ambiguity of both *knowing that* and *believing that,* resolving to keep our mode of interpretation constant or else to acknowledge appropriate adjustments in the prevalent definition.

KNOWING HOW AND BEING ABLE

We turn now to *procedural* knowledge, to *knowing how to.* By contrast with the propositional case, procedural knowing cannot be analyzed as involving truth, evidence, reasons, or belief—at least in *strictly parallel ways.* "X knows that _____" is completed by a full sentence, a propositional unit typically construable as a vehicle of belief, true or false, and well- or ill-grounded. "X knows how to _____" is not completed by a full sentence and does not bear *analogous* construction, though the *whole* statement, e.g., "X knows how to drive," *may of course* express belief, be true or false, and be well or ill grounded by available evidence.

Knowing how to represents the possession of a skill, a trained capacity, a competence, or a technique. We discussed skills earlier (in the second section of Chapter I) and distinguished them from traits, habits, or propensities, as well as from attainments—i.e., appreciation and understanding. Certainly having a skill is also quite different from knowing *that* the skill is such-and-such. A person might well have all the relevant information concerning some skill without having the skill itself, and conversely, he might be skilled without having any given piece of information concerning the skill in question, though it is unlikely he would lack *all* relevant information.

The relation between *knowing how* and *being able* is a complicated one, but we may perhaps hope to indicate some of its features here. First, the two notions are clearly not equivalent. A person may know how to drive but not be able to drive because, for example, he has a broken leg, or because his car has broken down. Conversely, we may judge a novice as being able to do a certain job though he does not yet know how. Furthermore, although the things we may sensibly be said to *know how* to do we may also sensibly be said to *be able* to do (given certain circumstances), the converse seems to fail. A person might, for example, sensibly be said to *be able* to tolerate a given dose of some drug without ever conceivably being said to *know how* to tolerate it. *Knowing how* seems relevant only to cases where *training* is at least minimally appropriate—that is, where repeated trial, or practice, is thought relevant to performance and where it is carried out under minimal conditions of understanding, which will be discussed later on.

There is a certain contextual variability in attributions of ability that seems impossible to eradicate. Take the example of the previous paragraph: a novice is being considered for a position requiring on-the-job training, say the position of teller in a bank. The bank manager may say of the girl, after an initial interview, that she seems *able* to do the job, although she does not, of course, yet know how. On the other hand, once she is hired and has embarked on her training course in the bank, the manager will think of her as *not* being able to take over a teller's window until she has completed her training and can be judged to know how to do the work. What accounts for such variability of judgment?

Perhaps the general situation can be represented as follows: A process or performance may be *prevented* through any of a variety of circumstances; to attribute *ability* in a given context typically amounts to denying that a preventive circumstance of a particular sort obtains, the sort being salient in context. To say, after my engine has been repaired, that I am now able to drive again may amount, in context, to saying that a defective engine no longer prevents my driving. To say the same thing after my broken arm has healed may rather be a way of indicating that my broken arm no longer prevents my driving; it would not normally be considered a refutation of my statement in the latter case to be told, for example, that my car had broken down again. In context, then, it would seem that an ability attribution typically serves to deny that some particular preventive circumstance obtains.

There is, to be sure, a limiting case of ability attribution, with which philosophers have often concerned themselves. Here, "absolute" ability is attributed to a person with respect to a performance, in the sense that all relevant preventive circumstances whatever are denied to hold and the performance judged to be contingent simply on the decision to perform in the requisite manner. There are notorious difficulties in the way of a precise analysis of "absolute" ability, but they need not concern us here. It will be sufficient for our purposes simply to acknowledge the concept of the limiting case and to note that the purported *absolute* sense should not be confused with the *contextual* use described earlier. Thus, when I say I am now able to drive again, meaning to assert only that a broken arm no longer prevents me from driving, it is not ruled out that I am still not "absolutely" able to drive. Both assertions are compatible, there being a difference between *contextual* attributions of ability and the limiting case of *absolute* attribution.

To say that a person *knows how* to do something is to make a certain sort of contextual ability attribution. It is to say that he is able to do it *in the special sense* that lack of training does not prevent him from doing it, although lack of training generally does constitute a preventive condition for things of this type. For a certain class of things, in other words, lack of training constitutes a preventive condition; in contexts where the supposition of *such* a preventive condition is at stake, the *know how* statement serves to negate it.

It can now be seen why, if it makes sense to describe a person as knowing how to do something, it also makes sense to describe him as able to do it (at least in certain circumstances), but not conversely. If he *knows how to* do a given thing, lack of training does not in his case stand in the way, although he may still not be "absolutely" able to do it because of some other preventive circumstance. Nevertheless, it may, in the context in question, be precisely the presumption of lack of training that requires rebuttal, in which case to say he *knows how* amounts to saying, in context, that he is *able*. It goes without saying that when, in a different context, some other preventive circumstance is at stake, its presumption may there be appropriately rebutted by another contextual ability attribution. On the other hand, if it is true that a person is *able to* do a given thing, it follows merely that its relevant preventive circumstances do not, in his case, stand in the way. But it does not at all follow that *lack of training* must be one of the preventive circumstances for things of this type. Lack of training does not generally prevent anyone from tolerating specific doses of certain drugs; we do not, therefore, say of anyone that he *knows how* to tolerate such a dose, although we may say that he is *able to* tolerate it, since relevant preventive conditions of other sorts are judged to fail in his case.

We may now interpret the variability of the manager's judgment in the case of the would-be bank teller. The manager initially judges the girl as *able* to perform the job of teller (though she does not yet *know how*), since she seems to lack generally preventive conditions (e.g., low intelligence, inadequate general schooling, etc.), conditions in respect of which initial applicants show variation, although they uniformly lack on-the-job training. Clearly, for the class of initial applicants, the mentioned variable preventive circumstances represent salient presumptions needing rebuttal. For the class of hired novices, on the other hand, these preventive circumstances have all been eliminated, variation now attaching primarily to the preventive condition represented by incomplete on-the-job training. When the manager judges the newly hired novice as not yet able to take over a teller's window, he is judging, in particular, that the newly relevant preventive circumstance of insufficient training has not yet been overcome. When he considers, finally, that the novice *is* now able to perform the teller's job, he judges that lack of training no longer stands in her way.

COMPETENCE, PROFICIENCY, AND MASTERY

We have remarked that *knowing how to* represents the possession of a skill, a trained capacity, a competence, or a technique. Earlier, we noted the general relevance of practice, skills being built up typically through training, in a gradual way, by means of repeated trials or performances. If the latter process is fairly continuous, at what point do we decide that the skill has been achieved? There is no general answer to this question, the same considerations holding here as were seen to be operative in appraising the adequacy of a person's evidence (see the second section of Chapter III). The standards we employ to decide when particular skills or competences have been reached vary analogously from context to context and will normally become more stringent with educational development. Attributions of skill or competence thus need to be interpreted in context.

On the other hand, the standard we use to specify a skill or competence in a given context need not eliminate *further* distinctions of relative proficiency or independent references to mastery or to greatness.[4] A person may be said to know how to play chess without being thereby asserted to be a good player, much less a master. Even when we define skills stringently—for example, in setting our own sights as teachers—we do not necessarily eliminate further gradations of "goodness" or proficiency, *some* of which may outstrip the estimated possibilities of training altogether. Though we may hope to bring children eventually to a high level of skill in chess-playing, we do not normally hope to make great players of them. Standards of achievement are, in a fundamental way, open-ended in the case of advanced skills. We need, however, to be aware of the *direction* in which greatness lies, and we need to give students an analogous awareness even though we cannot hope to train them to the point of greatness.

Not all skills are *advanced* skills, to be sure; for those that are not, the latter points do not seem to apply. We may still, of course, distinguish knowing how to spell from being a good speller, and knowing how to read from being a good reader. But we do not normally recognize any such things as genius, brilliance, or greatness in spelling or reading, as we do, for example, in chess, surgery, mathematics, or the violin. In the latter cases, the possibility of greater achievement always beckons, transcending even ideal specifications of *know how* for normal educational purposes. It is open-endedness of this sort which fits such capacities to absorb the continuing efforts and strivings of adults and to mark out directions for the growth of personality. The most we can do here, beyond developing know-how as far as is realistically possible, is to point to the direction of further achievement, sensitizing students so that they may recognize such achievement when it occurs and encouraging those who may be willing to strive for it. To sum up our main points, knowing how to do something is one thing, knowing how to do it well is, in general, another, and doing it brilliantly is still a third, which lies beyond the scope of *know how* altogether, tied as the latter notion is to the concept of training.

The force of these points will emerge more sharply through a general examination of Ryle's account of *knowing how*. Ryle's primary concern is with the theory of mind, his purpose to discredit the "intellectualist legend," which assimilates *knowing how* to *knowing that* by supposing that intelligent performance involves a prior intellectual acknowledgment of rules or criteria. According to the "intellectualist legend," says Ryle,

> The chef must recite his recipes to himself before he can cook according to them; the hero must lend his inner ear to some appropriate moral imperative before swimming out to save the drowning man; the chess-player must run over in his head all the relevant rules and tactical maxims of the game before he can make correct and skilful moves. To do something thinking what one is doing is, according to this legend, always to do two things; namely, to consider certain appropriate propositions, or prescriptions, and to put into practice what these propositions or prescriptions enjoin. It is to do a bit of theory and then to do a bit of practice (p. 29).[5]

Against this view, Ryle argues that "there are many classes of performances in which intelligence is displayed, but the rules or criteria of which are unformulated" (p. 30).

> The canons of aesthetic taste, of tactful manners and of inventive technique similarly remain unpropounded without impediment to the intelligent exercise of those gifts (p. 30).

He further argues that

> The consideration of propositions is itself an operation the execution of which can be more or less intelligent, less or more stupid. But if, for any operation to be intelligently executed, a prior theoretical operation had first to be performed and performed intelligently, it would be a logical impossibility for anyone ever to break into the circle (p. 30).

Finally, he contends that

> even where efficient practice is the deliberate application of considered prescriptions, the intelligence involved in putting the prescriptions into practice is not identical with that involved in intellectually grasping the prescriptions (p. 49).

In place of the "intellectualist legend," Ryle proposes that

> What distinguishes sensible from silly operations is not their parentage but their procedure, and this holds no less for intellectual than for practical performances. "Intelligent" cannot be defined in terms of "intellectual" or "knowing *how*" in terms of "knowing *that*"; "thinking what I am doing" does not connote "both thinking what to do and doing it". When I do something intelligently, i.e. thinking what I am doing, I am doing one thing and not two. My performance has a special procedure or manner, not special antecedents (p. 32).

How does this special manner or procedure reveal itself; how can it be described? Says Ryle,

> What is involved in our descriptions of people as knowing how to make and appreciate jokes, to talk grammatically, to play chess, to fish, or to argue? Part of what is meant is that, when they perform these operations, they tend to perform them well, i.e. correctly or efficiently or successfully. Their performances come up to certain standards, or satisfy certain criteria. But this is not enough. The well-regulated clock keeps good time and the well-drilled circus seal performs its tricks flawlessly, yet we do not call them "intelligent." We reserve this title for the persons responsible for these performances. To be intelligent is not merely to satisfy criteria, but to apply them; to regulate one's actions and not merely to be well-regulated. A person's performance is described as careful or skilful, if in his operations he is ready

to detect and correct lapses, to repeat and improve upon successes, to profit from the examples of others and so forth. He applies criteria in performing critically, that is, in trying to get things right. This point is commonly expressed in the vernacular by saying that an action exhibits intelligence, if, and only if, the agent is thinking what he is doing while he is doing it, and thinking what he is doing in such a manner that he would not do the action so well if he were not thinking what he is doing (pp. 28–29).

Let us first observe that Ryle equates *knowing how* with *intelligent performance,* with careful, skillful performance in which the agent would be commonly described as thinking what he is doing while he is doing it. Perhaps the main motivation for this equation is Ryle's preoccupation with refuting the "intellectualist legend," which prefaces *intelligent* performances, in particular, with cognitive apprehensions of appropriate sorts. In opposing this view, Ryle is primarily concerned to put forth an alternative conception of *intelligence,* as displayed in the manner of the performance itself rather than in its antecedents. This is an important conception, surely, and deserves independent consideration to determine whether or not it is, in the final analysis, superior to its "intellectualist" rival. However that may be, Ryle's incidental assimilation of *knowing how* to *intelligent performance,* though understandable, is surely dubious, as has already been intimated in our earlier discussion.

For *know how* covers not merely what we might call (in the spirit of Ryle's treatment) *critical skills,* but also relatively routinizable or automatic competences, such as spelling, which, once attained, normally require no critical effort in performance: we do not have a category of intelligent spelling. Further, even in the case of skills not thus routinizable, attribution of *intelligence* normally goes beyond mere attribution of *know how:* to read, or play chess, intelligently is more than just to know how to read, or how to play. The operative criterion for knowing how to play, for example, is indeed variable, and we may, in given contexts, wish to withhold the attribution of *know how* from the student until a certain level of intelligent play is attained. But such a decision is not forced on us, and we may well construe intelligent play as a further condition beyond the achievement of a minimal strategic know-how; indeed, such a construal is perhaps typical in the case of chess, except perhaps when we are speaking in ideal terms, in setting our own curricular sights over the long term. By taking *know-how* as *intelligent performance,* Ryle thus considerably narrows its full range, excluding altogether the routinizable (noncritical) competences, on the one hand, and minimal achievement of the critical (nonroutinizable) competences, on the other. It will be worth looking more closely at the chess example, for both points of exclusion may be illustrated by it. Let us consider the latter exclusion first. We have indicated a difference between knowing how to play chess and playing it intelligently. The player displays intelligence primarily in his strategy. He has to choose among alternative moves, all permissible by the constitutive rules of the game. There is no comparable occasion for choice in spelling nor, comparably, any element of strategy that enters into the spelling task. Practically available principles of chess strategy are, moreover, flexible and incomplete; they do not guarantee success to those who take them into account. Proficiency in chess is, accordingly, not increased through routinization; a critical skill such as chess is quite different from capacities in which increased proficiency does result from increased routinization. Just the latter sort of contrast leads Ryle to introduce the notion "intelligent capacity" and to oppose it to "habit" (p. 42). But here we must note the crucial point: To label a *capacity* "intelligent" because it calls for strategic judgment does *not* imply that everyone who *has* the capacity displays intelligence in the *exercise* of it, i.e., shows *good* strategic judgment. It is no contradiction to say that a person has acquired an "intelligent capacity" such as chess (that is, has learned how to play) but does not show intelligence in the way he exercises it (that is, does not play well, carefully, skillfully, or successfully).

The exclusion by Ryle of routinizable (noncritical) competences from the realm of *know-how* is, if anything, more striking than the sort of exclusion we have just discussed. Chess will here again serve us as an illustration if we reflect that even the minimal strategic sophistication normally associated with bare know-how is built on the capacity to operate in accordance with the constitutive rules defining permissible moves in the game. Certainly one may be said to know how to move the chessmen properly; this bit of know-how is, indeed, an essential ingredient, though not the whole, of knowing how to play. Yet it *is* routinizable, every possible move on the board being determined by the constitutive rules to be either a proper move—i.e., permitted—or not. Strategy in chess presupposes awareness of such propriety; there is no prior set of strategic principles guiding decisions as to propriety. Indeed the latter decisions do need to become relatively automatic if the student is really to be said to have the relevant know-how. In any event, it is clear that he need not, at *this* level, fulfill the conditions stipulated by Ryle for *knowing how*—namely, thinking what he is doing while doing it, exercising care, standing ready to repeat and improve upon successes and to profit from the examples of others.

In one passage, Ryle does indeed try to bring considerations of chess "propriety" under the rubric of know-how, at least by implication. He is arguing, in this passage, that one does not know how to play if all that one can do is to recite the rules. "But," he continues, "he is said to know how to play if, although he cannot cite the rules, he normally does make the permitted moves, avoid the forbidden moves and protest if his opponent makes forbidden moves" (p. 41). This seems, however, to conflict with Ryle's own theoretical account of "knowing how" as intelligent performance. For, surely, no one who knows how to play chess needs to expend judgment in deciding whether a piece is being properly moved, nor does he "exercise care, vigilance, or criticism" (p. 42) in the process, thinking what he is doing all the while, "so that every operation performed is itself a new lesson to him how to perform better" (p. 43). Ryle's theoretical account is after all, as we have argued, too narrow; in using the present chess illustration, he provides a counterexample to his own theory. Somewhat the same point might be made about his reference to "knowing how" to talk grammatically, in the same breath with knowing how to argue (p. 28).

Grammatical talk, like observance of chess propriety, is an ingredient of intelligent performance. It is a bit of know-how nested within another, more complex, bit of know-how. Nonetheless, it is not itself of the same order, being removed from the sphere of critical judgment, which focusses on the whole. Artistic technique provides another class of relevant examples and Dewey's remark is here germane: "The artist is a masterful technician. The technique or mechanism is fused with thought and feeling. The 'mechanical' performer permits the mechanism to dictate the performance. It is absurd to say that the latter exhibits habit and the former not. We are confronted with two kinds of habit, intelligent and routine."[6] Judgment is exercised, as Dewey would have it, in control of the *whole* performance, but this does not imply that the artist must therefore expend judgment in deciding each note. Nevertheless, his underlying technique represents a competence: a bit of know-how. Relatively routinizable competences of the sorts we have discussed (including also e.g., typing, computation, etc.) we shall call *facilities,* our argument being that *both* facilities *and* critical skills (Ryle's "intelligent capacities") belong to the realm of know-how.

Earlier we suggested that Ryle's main motivation for emphasizing critical skills is his preoccupation with refuting the "intellectualist legend." A secondary motivation may be represented by the wish to contrast genuine *knowing how* with the activity of the well-regulated clock and the well-drilled circus seal. If our earlier discussion (in the second section of this Chapter) is correct, however, there will surely be no problem in distinguishing facilities from the activity of clocks. For facilities, like critical skills, are abilities *acquired through training*. They are acquired, that is, through a variety of procedures involving repeated trials and including, or at least capable of being facilitated by, the process of *showing how*, by description, explanation, or example. This is a minimal, though crucial, element of *understanding or communication*, which differentiates even an automatic typing facility, for example, from the time-telling of a clock. As to the performance of the seal, much depends on the view taken of its learning; if we allow that *training* is genuinely involved, it does not seem at all obvious that the seal must be denied to *know how* to perform its tricks. There will, in any event, always be borderline cases difficult to decide, and it is sufficient if an analysis avoids clear counterexamples.

CRITICAL SKILL AND THE AMBIGUITY OF "PRACTICE"

We have been urging a broad construction of *knowing how to*, which does not limit it to cases of intelligent performance. We have, however, acknowledged a distinction between facilities and critical skills, on the ground that the former but not the latter are relatively routinizable, the latter involving always an ineliminable engagement of judgment in the performance.

This distinction underlies Ryle's contrast of "intelligent capacities" with "habits." He writes,

> The ability to give by rote the correct solutions of multiplication problems differs in certain important respects from the ability to solve them by calculating. When we describe someone as doing something by pure or blind habit, we mean that he does it automatically and without having to mind what he is doing. He does not exercise care, vigilance, or criticism. After the toddling-age we walk on pavements without minding our steps. But a mountaineer walking over ice-covered rocks in a high wind in the dark does not move his limbs by blind habit; he thinks what he is doing, he is ready for emergencies, he economises in effort, he makes tests and experiments; in short he walks with some degree of skill and judgment. If he makes a mistake, he is inclined not to repeat it, and if he finds a new trick effective he is inclined to continue to use it and to improve on it. He is concomitantly walking and teaching himself how to walk in conditions of this sort. It is of the essence of merely habitual practices that one performance is a replica of its predecessors. It is of the essence of intelligent practices that one performance is modified by its predecessors. The agent is still learning (p. 42).

Ryle's account, taken as a characterization of intelligent capacities, or what we have called *critical skills*, is surely well taken. But the contrast he makes with *habit* is misleading, for he includes under *habit* not only facilities such as "the ability to give by rote the correct solutions of multiplication problems" (p. 42) but also "the smoking habit of a man" (p. 43), which is no ability at all, hence not a facility, but rather a proneness or propensity. "My being an habitual smoker," he writes, "does not entail that I am at this or that moment smoking; it is my permanent proneness to smoke when I am not eating, sleeping, lecturing or attending funerals, and have not quite recently been smoking" (p. 43). Propensities are clearly quite different from abilities; no normal person, for example, is thought to have the permanent *proneness* to give by rote the correct solution of multiplication problems though many are considered to have the *ability;* while having the smoking habit is clearly more than having the practical ability to light up. Propensities do not belong to the realm of know-how though they may presuppose know-how. Perhaps it is Ryle's grouping of propensities with facilities that provides still another cause for his exclusion of the latter from the sphere of *knowing how to.* At any rate, as we have argued above, facilities *should* be included within this sphere, though they share certain common properties with the excluded habitual propensities—in particular, the possibility of being rendered automatic.

Ryle makes two further distinctions between intelligent capacities and habits: first, that the former, though not the latter, are always multiple-track dispositions, "the exercises of which are indefinitely heterogeneous" (p. 44), and secondly, that habits are built up by drill whereas intelligent capacities are built up by training. This second distinction is of considerable interest from an educational point of view.

Drill is taken to be "the imposition of repetitions." Ryle continues,

> The recruit learns to slope arms by repeatedly going through just the same motions by numbers. The child learns the alphabet and the multiplication tables in the same way. The practices are not learned until the pupil's responses to his cues are automatic, until he can "do them in his sleep," as it is revealingly put. Training, on the other hand, though it embodies plenty of sheer drill, does not consist of drill. It involves the stimulation by criticism and example of the pupil's own judgment. He learns how to do things thinking what he is doing, so that every operation performed is itself a new lesson to him how to perform better. The soldier who

was merely drilled to slope arms correctly has to be trained to be proficient in marksmanship and map-reading. Drill dispenses with intelligence, training develops it. We do not expect the soldier to be able to read maps "in his sleep" (pp. 42–43).

The distinction made here is of general importance for the concept of *knowing how to*. For, as we have noted earlier, skills and competences are generally developed through *practice*, through *repeated trial or performance*. But the latter notions are capable of quite different constructions. They may be taken to approximate drill, on the one hand, in which unthinking repetition is the rule, or they may be taken, on the other hand, to involve opportunities for engaging the student's judgment and for refining it through criticism and evaluation of its consequences. As we noted in discussing the case of chess, critical skills call for strategic judgment and cannot be rendered automatic. To construe the learning of chess as a matter of drill would thus be quite wrong-headed in suggesting that the same game be played over and over again, or intimating that going through the motions of playing repeatedly somehow improves one's game. What is rather supposed, at least in the case of chess, is that improvement comes about through development of strategic judgment, which requires that such judgment be allowed opportunity to guide choices in a wide variety of games, with maximal opportunity for evaluating relevant outcomes and reflecting upon alternative principles of strategy in the light of such evaluation.

The ambiguity of *practice* is thus of paramount importance in the education of skill. It is, for example, of critical importance in professional education, for the doctor, the researcher, the lawyer, and the teacher are not simply persons who have acquired technical facilities which can be run off automatically; they need competences which require the continual exercise of strategic judgment concerning individual cases which they have never confronted before and for which there are no exhaustive rules dictating decisions to be made. *Practice* in professional education is thus misconceived if assimilated to the model of drill or to the repeated study of standard cases. There needs to be room for training opportunities which will provide for the genuine exercise of students' judgment, as well as for critical reflection on the outcomes and strategic principles of such judgment.

One important general implication of the emphasis on *critical* practice is that performance and intelligence do not belong in strictly separated compartments. Many thinkers have, in fact, supposed that performance is generally routine and habitual while intelligence is, strictly speaking, spontaneous and innovative, the main function of education being to automatize performance so that the mind may be set free. Even so sensitive a psychological theorist as William James supports, or at least suggests, such a view.

> Habit diminishes the conscious attention with which our acts are performed. . . . The great thing, then, in all education, is to *make our nervous system our ally instead of our enemy.* It is to fund and capitalize our acquisitions, and live at ease upon the interest of the fund. *For this we must make automatic and habitual, as early as possible, as many useful actions as we can,* and guard against the growing into ways that are likely to be disadvantageous to us, as we should guard against the plague. The more of the details of our daily life we can hand over to the effortless custody of automatism, the more our higher powers of mind will be set free for their own proper work.[7]

There is much truth in this view, but the doubtful suggestion, by omission, is that performance is *generally* capable of becoming routinized. Ryle's emphasis on "intelligent capacities" has the virtue that it clearly gives the chief place to performance which cannot be thus routinized, since it calls for judgment in its very execution and is improvable only to the extent that it is refined by intelligence in a continual process of learning. In this fusion of performance and intelligence, he approximates Dewey's view in the passage cited earlier, in the third section of the present Chapter. Whereas, however, Dewey achieves his fusion by using *habit* in such a broad sense that even artistic skill becomes a habit, as we have seen, Ryle preserves a special role for habits as automatic and capable of development through sheer drill, meanwhile introducing a contrasting and fused category: that of intelligent performance or know-how.

Our own view has been rather that habits (as propensities) need to be distinguished from facilities, the latter clearly belonging to the sphere of know-how. We have urged a further distinction between both of these and critical skills. We have, however, acknowledged that nested within the latter are facilities of various sorts which *may* call for different methods of development from those appropriate for the critical skills as wholes.

One important point concerning development needs to be dealt with. Ryle opposes *training* to *drill* and supposes that facilities are built up through drill, construed as a mere "imposition of repetitions." We have earlier argued, to the contrary, that facilities, like critical skills, are developed through *training,* which always involves, at least in a minimal way, the notion of *understanding.* Practice in the sense of *drill,* and *critical* practice may both, in our view, be *involved in* the process of training. Training, however, always involves understanding, in the minimal sense earlier discussed.

What is it that leads Ryle to say that facilities are built up by drill? Surely his reason must be that facilities are routinizable, becoming increasingly automatic as they are developed. This does *not*, however, *at all* imply that drill alone is capable of building them up. Once they are developed, they are indeed automatic and repetitive; it cannot be inferred that they are therefore *acquired* in an automatic and repetitive way. In the case of intelligent capacities, the agent is always, as Ryle says, still learning. It does not, however, follow that because this is *not* true for facilities, the agent is *never* (in the same sense) learning. "After the toddling-age," says Ryle, "we walk on pavements without minding our steps." But then during the toddling-age we *do* mind our steps, and drill is, at least at this stage, inappropriate. It cannot thus be the exclusive method for developing facilities. Drill is actually, I should suggest, a sophisticated method in this and similar cases. Though it surely has a place in developing facility, the relevance of *showing how*, through description, example, or explanation, is never ruled out; it may be of special importance in early stages of learning, but it never altogether loses its significance for the process. The potential relevance of insight, questioning, understanding, and communication remains, indeed, even in cases where drill is the chief need of the moment. Such relevance is an index of the intellectual character of procedural, as of propositional, knowledge.

•

Intellect and Rationality

•

In Chapter II, we stressed the fact that educational notions have a *wider* range than that of "knowing," embracing also habits, traits, propensities of one or another sort, and attainments. However, in our primary concern with the overlapping regions of theory of knowledge and philosophy of education, we subsequently stayed within the bounds of the concept of knowing and did not attempt a general treatment of educational ideas. While this restriction was quite proper in view of the main purpose of our discussions, a parting word must here be addressed to the larger scope of educational concepts —in particular, the concept of teaching.

This parting word is especially needed in view of the distinction we made in the last chapter between habitual propensities and facilities, admitting only the latter to the realm of "know-how" and stressing the intellectual elements of procedural, as well as propositional, knowledge. For it might have been suggested, wrongly, that *rationality* is itself bound to the concept of *knowledge* and has no application outside the sphere of "knowing that" and "knowing how." Nothing could be further from the truth.

We have seen (in the last chapter) the difficulty of restricting the concept of intellect to "knowing that," and taking it to be the primary element in intelligent exercise of skill. But neither intellect nor intelligence, nor their combination, itself exhausts the scope of *rationality,* and it is the latter concept to which teaching is closely tied.

We have earlier (in Chapter I) stressed the association of "teaching" with rational explanation and critical dialogue, arguing that the teacher's genuine engagement in such dialogue marks the characteristic *manner* of teaching. The heart of the enterprise is, as we have said, the giving of honest reasons and the welcoming of radical questions, a sort of interaction which exposes the teacher's underlying judgment to the critical evaluation of the student, and invites the student to form and submit his own judgments likewise to critical appraisal.

Rationality is coextensive with the relevance of reasons. Where *beliefs* are in question, reasons pertain to evidence or credible supporting assumptions of the sorts we discussed in Chapter III. Where skills are involved, reasons pertain to the basis for following one procedure rather than another, choosing one rather than another step or strategy, or building up such-and-such a facility rather than another for the sake of achieving a given broad competence. Reasons may also be requested for the implicit value placed upon the skill in question. *Showing how*, to be sure, is not in every case a matter of giving reasons, but may proceed, for instance, through providing examples for imitation. ("Training," though it involves understanding, does not yet carry the *full* connotations of "teaching.") Nonetheless, reasons *may* be requested for the particular way in which a competence is structured or for its valuation, as suggested above. (Training may itself be embedded in an enterprise of genuine teaching.)

Now where propensities, habits, traits, and even attainments are concerned, reasons are surely also involved in the latter sense—that is, in purportedly justifying the valuations which are implicit in the teaching of these propensities, habits, traits, and attainments. What purposes lie behind their choice as elements of educational content? What are the considerations by which their worthwhileness might be made out and what are the counterconsiderations? These questions of *value* and *purpose* are surely relevant here and must indeed be judged to be legitimate and important from the standpoint of rationality defining the *manner* distinctive of teaching.

Rationality is thus a much broader notion than that of intellect, or even intelligence in performance, and defines a much *wider* educational ideal. For unless we arbitrarily restrict education to the sphere of knowledge, we must admit that the formation of habits, character, propensities, and attainments falls within its scope and that it may be conducted in rational spirit, through teaching, or in manipulative spirit, through a whole battery of old and new technological devices for shaping mind and behavior.

We have, in this book, been largely concerned with intellect and skill, but these notions are too specialized to serve as overarching educational concepts. For such a concept we may turn to "teaching," as connoting an initiation into the rational life, a life in which the critical quest for reasons is a dominant and integrating motive.

FOOTNOTES

INTRODUCTION

1. Each of the three sketches to follow is a composite, but it may be helpful to associate some names with the approaches treated. With rationalism we may associate Plato, Descartes, and Leibniz; with empiricism, Locke, Berkeley, and Hume; with pragmatism, Peirce, James, and Dewey.

2. Briefly, the point may be illustrated by this figure.

The problem is to determine what square is twice the area of the shaded square. The boy is led to see that the large square made by doubling the side of the shaded square yields a figure of four times the area, which is itself halved by the internal square made up of the diagonals, since each diagonal cuts its small containing square in half. The conclusion is that the square of the diagonal of the shaded square has double the area of the latter.

3. John Dewey, *Democracy and Education* (New York: The Macmillan Company, 1916, Paperbacks Edition, 1961), p. 139.

CHAPTER ONE

1. The letter *Q* occurs here, and in discussions to follow, sometimes framed by quotation marks, sometimes not. The letter *without* quo-

tation marks stands in place of a sentence, fully displayed at the location of the occurrence in question. The letter *with* quotation marks, on the other hand, stands in place of a name of the sentence in question—typically, in place of the sentence-name which consists of the sentence itself framed by quotes.

2. For example, Jaakko Hintikka, *Knowledge and Belief* (Ithaca, N.Y.: Cornell University Press, 1962), pp. 18–19.

3. On this point, see Israel Scheffler, *The Language of Education* (Springfield, Ill.: Charles C. Thomas, 1960), pp. 42, 60–61.

4. The criticisms of Marcus Brown, "Knowing and learning," *Harvard Educational Review*, XXXI (Winter 1961), 10–11, and note 19, thus seem to me to be taken care of.

5. See Scheffler, *The Language of Education*, p. 98.

6. Variants of this definition may be found in Roderick M. Chisholm, *Perceiving: A Philosophical Study* (Ithaca, N.Y.: Cornell University Press, 1957), p. 16, and in D. J. O'Connor, *An Introduction to the Philosophy of Education* (New York: Philosophical Library, 1957), p. 73.

CHAPTER TWO

1. Roderick M. Chisholm, *Perceiving: A Philosophical Study* (Ithaca, N.Y.: Cornell University Press, 1957), pp. 17–18.

2. J. L. Austin, "Other Minds," *Philosophical Papers* (Oxford at the Clarendon Press, 1961), p. 67. The paper originally appeared in Supplementary Volume XX of *Proceed-*

ings of the Aristotelian Society (1946). Page references to Austin in the text relate to his *Philosophical Papers* throughout.

3. Gilbert Ryle, *The Concept of Mind* (London: Hutchinson House, 1949). The discussion of category-mistakes begins on p. 16. Page references to Ryle in the text relate to *The Concept of Mind* throughout.

4. *An Enquiry Concerning Human Understanding*, Section II.

5. David Hume, *A Treatise of Human Nature*, Book I, Part I, Section VI.

6. *An Enquiry Concerning Human Understanding*, Section II.

7. On these issues see Clarence Irving Lewis, *An Analysis of Knowledge and Valuation* (La Salle, Ill.: The Open Court Publishing Company, 1946), Book II, especially Chapter VII; Alfred J. Ayer, *The Foundations of Empirical Knowledge* (New York: St. Martin's Press, 1961); and the survey in Arthur Pap, *Elements of Analytic Philosophy* (New York: The Macmillan Company, 1949), Chapters 7 and 8. An excellent discussion may be found in the symposium by C. I. Lewis, Hans Reichenbach, and Nelson Goodman, "The Experiential Element in Knowledge," *Philosophical Review*, LXI (April 1952), 147–175.

8. For a discussion of this idea see A. J. Ayer, *The Problem of Knowledge* (Harmondsworth: Penguin Books, Ltd., 1956), pp. 54–57. The whole of Ayer's Chapter 2 is also of considerable interest.

9. See Austin, *Philosophical Papers*, p. 58 ff.

10. See Nelson Goodman, "Sense and Certainty," *Philosophical Review*, LXI (April 1952), 160–167.

11. Aside from the *Collected Papers of Charles S. Peirce* (Vols. 1–6, ed. Hartshorne and Weiss; Cambridge, Mass.: Harvard University Press, 1931–1935; and vols. 7–8, ed. Burks; Cambridge, Mass.: Harvard University Press, 1958), there are several single-volume collections of Peirce's major papers. One of the most useful of these is the recent *Values in a Universe of Chance: Selected Writings of Charles S. Peirce*, edited by Philip P. Wiener (New York: Doubleday, 1958; also Stanford: Stanford University Press, 1958). Page references to Peirce in the present book will thus relate to Wiener's collection throughout. (Our citations are first to Peirce's essay "How to Make Our Ideas Clear" [pp. 113–136 in Wiener] and later to Peirce's essay "The Fixation of Belief" [pp. 91–112 in Wiener]. Both essays first appeared in *Popular Science Monthly*, the latter in November 1877, the former in January 1878). W. B. Gallie, *Peirce and Pragmatism* (Harmondsworth: Penguin Books, Ltd., 1952) may be recommended as a lucid introduction and commentary.

12. For operationism, see P. W. Bridgman, *The Logic of Modern Physics* (New York: The Macmillan Company, 1927). A recent symposium discussion, "The Present State of Operationalism," is contained in Philipp G. Frank, *The Validation of Scientific Theories* (Boston: The Beacon Press, 1956).

13. Recent criticisms of this account with which we shall not deal here are found in Willard Van Orman Quine, *Word and Object* (New York: The Technology Press of the Massachusetts Institute of Technology; also John Wiley & Sons, Inc., 1960), p. 23.

14. See Morton White, *The Age of Analysis* (New York: Mentor Books, 1955), pp. 154–160.

15. William James, *Pragmatism* (New York: Longmans, Green and Co., 1910), p. 58. Page references to James in the text relate to this book throughout.

16. Some points in my criticism of James in the text are developed from comments in my review of Morton White's *Toward Reunion in Philosophy, Harvard Educational Review*, XXVII (Spring 1957), 156–158. Aside from the writings of Tarski and Carnap, to be noted shortly in the text and to which my critical remarks are indebted, I want to call special attention to the incisive critique, "William James' Pragmatism," by G. E. Moore, included in the latter's *Philosophical Studies* (New York: Harcourt, Brace & Co., 1922). It is perhaps of some interest to note that Peirce, in the last sentence of his "A Neglected Argument for the Reality of God," deplores James' notion of the mutability of truth as a "seed of death" that has been allowed to infect pragmatism, a "philosophy so instinct with life" (p. 379).

17. See in this connection, A. Koyré, "Galilée et l'Expérience de Pise," *Annales de l'Université de Paris* (1937), pp. 441–453; and Herbert Butterfield, *The Origins of Modern Science* (New York: The Macmillan Company, Paperbacks Edition, 1960), pp. 81–82.

18. See Nelson Goodman, *The Structure of Appearance* (Cambridge, Mass.: Harvard University Press, 1951), pp. 287 ff. for a systematic treatment of indicators.

19. Alfred Tarski, "The Semantic Conception of Truth," *Philosophy and Phenomenological Research* (1944). Reprinted in Herbert Feigl and Wilfrid Sellars, *Readings in Philosophical Analysis* (New York: Appleton-Century-Crofts, Inc., 1949), pp. 52–84.

20. Rudolf Carnap, "Truth and Confirmation," in Feigl and Sellars, pp. 119–127.

21. Aristotle, *Metaphysics*, Book IV, Chapter 7.

22. Feigl and Sellars, *Readings in Philosophical Analysis*, p. 54.

23. Feigl and Sellars, p. 71.

24. Willard Van Orman Quine, *From a Logical Point of View* (Cambridge, Mass.: Harvard University Press, 1953), p. 138. See Chapter VII of this book for further discussion of the semantic conception.

25. Feigl and Sellars, *Readings in Philosophical Analysis* p. 123.

26. Feigl and Sellars, p. 123.

CHAPTER THREE
1. Saint Augustine, "The Teacher," included in Kingsley Price, *Education and Philosophical Thought* (Boston: Allyn and Bacon, Inc., 1962). Page references to Augustine in the text relate to "The Teacher" in *Education and Philosophical Thought* throughout.

2. See Alfred North Whitehead,

The Aims of Education (New York: The Macmillan Company, 1929), Chapter 2, "The Rhythm of Education."

3. On this point, see Nelson Goodman, "Sense and Certainty," *Philosophical Review* LXI (April 1952), 160–167.

4. J. L. Austin, *Philosophical Papers* (Oxford at the Clarendon Press, 1961). Page references to Austin relate to his *Philosophical Papers* throughout.

5. A. J. Ayer, *The Problem of Knowledge* (Harmondsworth: Penguin Books, Ltd., 1956), Chapter 1, especially pp. 31–35.

6. Ayer, p. 35. On the issue of "subjective certainty" see the interesting papers of A. D. Woozley, "Knowing and Not Knowing," *Proceeding of the Aristotelian Society,* LIII (1953), 151–172; and L. J. Cohen, "Claims to Knowledge," *Proceedings of the Aristotelian Society,* Supplementary Vol. XXXVI (1962), 33–50.

7. See Willard Van Orman Quine, *Methods of Logic* (New York: Henry Holt & Company, 1950), pp. 190–191.

8. Included in Henri Poincaré, *Science and Method,* trans. Francis Maitland (New York: Dover Publications, Inc., 1952), pp. 117–142. Page references to Poincaré in the text relate to "Mathematical Definitions and Education" throughout.

CHAPTER FOUR

1. Rudolf Carnap, *Meaning and Necessity* (Chicago: The University of Chicago Press, 1947), Sections 13–15, pp. 53–64.

2. The context of systematic questioning is suggested in Carnap, pp. 53–4.

3. R. M. Hare, *The Language of Morals* (Oxford at the Clarendon Press, 1952), p. 60.

4. Hare, p. 60.

5. B. F. Skinner, *Verbal Behavior* (New York: Appleton-Century-Crofts, Inc., 1957), pp. 362–365.

6. See Kingsley Price, "On 'Having an Education,' " *Harvard Educational Review,* XXVIII (Fall 1958), 330 ff.; and R. M. Chisholm, *Perceiving: A Philosophical Study* (Ithaca, New York: Cornell University Press, 1957), p. 15. Chisholm's remarks are critical of the attempt to reduce *knowing that* to a verbal sort of *knowing how,* as in John Hartland-Swann, "The Logical Status of 'Knowing That,' " *Analysis,* XVI (1956), 114.

7. N. Chomsky, "Review of B. F. Skinner, *Verbal Behavior,*" *Language,* XXXV (1959), 26–58, footnote 43.

8. Gilbert Ryle, *The Concept of Mind* (London: Hutchinson House, 1949). Page references to Ryle in the text relate to *The Concept of Mind* throughout.

9. Carl G. Hempel, "Rational Action," *Proceedings and Addresses of the American Philosophical Association* XXXV (Yellow Springs, Ohio: The Antioch Press, 1962), pp. 5–23. Page references to Hempel in the text relate to this article throughout.

10. See Israel Scheffler, *The Language of Education* (Springfield, Ill.:

Charles C. Thomas, 1960), pp. 57, 68.

CHAPTER FIVE

1. On the sufficiency of the conditions laid down by the definition, see Bertrand Russell, *Human Knowledge: Its Scope and Limits* (New York: Simon and Schuster, 1948), pp. 154–155; Edmund L. Gettier, "Is Justified True Belief Knowledge?," *Analysis*, XXIII (June 1963), 121–123; and Michael Clark, "Knowledge and Grounds: A Comment on Mr. Gettier's Paper," *Analysis*, XXIV (December 1963), 46–48.

Russell's example (though he does not himself develop it in this way) is as follows: A man "looks at a clock which is not going, though he thinks it is, and . . . happens to look at it the moment when it is right." He acquires a true belief as to the time, which is, moreover, *justified*, if we assume he has good grounds to suppose the clock *is* going. Yet it seems wrong to hold that he *knows* that it is (say) three o'clock. Shall we, perhaps, tighten the requirements so as to demand that his intermediate assumption of the clock's proper functioning be *true*; or shall we allow that the man does know it is three o'clock, but simply deny the normal presumption that he likewise knows the clock to *be* functioning properly? Or is some other approach preferable?

2. Israel Scheffler, *The Language of Education* (Springfield, Ill.: Charles C. Thomas, 1960), p. 79.

3. Scheffler, p. 79 ff.

4. Scheffler, p. 43.

5. Gilbert Ryle, *The Concept of Mind* (London: Hutchinson House, 1949). Page references to Ryle in the text relate to *The Concept of Mind* throughout.

6. John Dewey, *Human Nature and Conduct* (New York: The Modern Library, 1930), p. 71.

7. William James, *The Principles of Psychology*, Vol. I (New York: Dover Publications, Inc. Reprinted by special arrangement with Henry Holt and Company, 1950), 114, 122.

BIBLIOGRAPHY

Austin, J. L. *Philosophical Papers.* Oxford at the Clarendon Press, 1961.
A collection of acute and influential papers by one of the leaders of recent English philosophy. Difficult for the beginner.

Ayer, A. J. *The Problem of Knowledge.* Harmondsworth, Penguin Books, Ltd., 1956
An excellent general account, accessible to the beginner.

Chisholm, R. M. *Perceiving: A Philosophical Study.* Ithaca, N.Y., Cornell University Press, 1957.
Acute discussions of problems of perception and intention.

Flew, A. *Essays in Conceptual Analysis.* London, Macmillan & Co., Ltd., 1960.
Anthology of selections of recent analytic philosophy, many of which relate to epistemological issues.

Hartland-Swann, J. *An Analysis of Knowing.* London, Ruskin House, George Allen & Unwin, Ltd., 1958.
A readable, short book dealing with many of the areas I have touched on.

Hintikka, J. *Knowledge and Belief.* Ithaca, N.Y., Cornell University Press, 1962.
A recent, relatively difficult treatise on the logical problems of knowledge and belief.

Lewis, C. I. *An Analysis of Knowledge and Valuation.* La Salle, Ill.: The Open Court Publishing Company, 1946.
A major systematic treatise by an important American philosopher. Somewhat difficult for the beginner, but well worth the effort.

Macdonald, M., ed., *Philosophy and Analysis.* New York, Philosophical Library, Inc., 1954.
A collection of papers that originally appeared in the English philosophical journal, *Analysis.* Several are relevant to the topics of knowledge, belief, meaning, and truth.

Malcolm, N. *Knowledge and Certainty; Essays and Lectures.* Englewood Cliffs, N.J., Prentice-Hall, Inc., 1963.
Important papers by a contemporary American philosopher.

Moore, G. E. *Philosophical Studies.* New York, Harcourt, Brace & Co., Inc., 1922.
Papers by one of the founders of contemporary analytic philosophy. Difficult for the beginner.

Moore, G. E. *Some Main Problems of Philosophy.* New York, The Macmillan Company, 1953.
Papers by one of the founders of contemporary analytic philosophy. Difficult for the beginner.

Polanyi, M. *Personal Knowledge.* Chicago, University of Chicago Press, 1958. A provocative recent treatise emphasizing the personal element in scientific knowledge.

Russell, B. *Human Knowledge: Its Scope and Limits.* New York: Simon and Schuster, 1948. A general treatise by an outstanding logician and philosopher, dealing with many of the issues touched on here.

Woozley, A. D. *Theory of Knowledge: An Introduction.* London, Hutchinson & Company, 1960. An excellent little introduction to the problems; can be read by the beginner.